Cambridge Elements

Elements in Gender and Politics
edited by
Tiffany D. Barnes
University of Texas at Austin
Diana Z. O'Brien
Washington University in St. Louis

DOUBLE GLASS CEILING

The Class Effects of Gender Representation

Jeong Hyun Kim
Yonsei University

Yesola Kweon
Sungkyunkwan University

Shaftesbury Road, Cambridge CB2 8EA, United Kingdom

One Liberty Plaza, 20th Floor, New York, NY 10006, USA

477 Williamstown Road, Port Melbourne, VIC 3207, Australia

314–321, 3rd Floor, Plot 3, Splendor Forum, Jasola District Centre, New Delhi – 110025, India

Cambridge University Press is part of Cambridge University Press & Assessment, a department of the University of Cambridge.

We share the University's mission to contribute to society through the pursuit of education, learning and research at the highest international levels of excellence.

www.cambridge.org
Information on this title: www.cambridge.org/9781009461054

DOI: 10.1017/9781009461030

© Jeong Hyun Kim and Yesola Kweon 2026

This publication is in copyright. Subject to statutory exception and to the provisions of relevant collective licensing agreements, no reproduction of any part may take place without the written permission of Cambridge University Press & Assessment.

When citing this work, please include a reference to the DOI 10.1017/9781009461030

First published 2026

A catalogue record for this publication is available from the British Library

ISBN 978-1-009-46105-4 Hardback
ISBN 978-1-009-46104-7 Paperback
ISSN 2753-8117 (online)
ISSN 2753-8109 (print)

Additional resources for this publication at www.Cambridge.org/Kim/Kweon

Cambridge University Press & Assessment has no responsibility for the persistence or accuracy of URLs for external or third-party internet websites referred to in this publication and does not guarantee that any content on such websites is, or will remain, accurate or appropriate.

For EU product safety concerns, contact us at Calle de José Abascal, 56, 1°, 28003 Madrid, Spain, or email eugpsr@cambridge.org

Double Glass Ceiling

The Class Effects of Gender Representation

Elements in Gender and Politics

DOI: 10.1017/9781009461030
First published online: January 2026

Jeong Hyun Kim
Yonsei University

Yesola Kweon
Sungkyunkwan University

Author for correspondence: Yesola Kweon, yesola.kweon@skku.edu

> **Abstract:** This Element sheds light on the intersectionality of class and gender in political representation. Although the working class is grossly underrepresented in most legislative bodies across the globe, the underrepresentation of the working class is particularly severe among female representatives. This Element examines the political significance of the shortage of working-class women in political bodies. Specifically, it argues that the link between women's descriptive and symbolic representation will appear differently across economic class, which could, in turn, have significant implications for working-class women's political attitudes and behavior. The Element first theorizes and empirically tests the class-based differences in women's policy priorities. Next, it studies how the class-based representation gap in politics might undermine a sense of political efficacy among women from underprivileged backgrounds. Taken together, the theory and findings of this Element make vital contributions to gender and politics research by uncovering the class- and gender-based dynamics in political representation.

Keywords: Gender and class, democratic representation, policy priorities, political efficacy, political engagement

© Jeong Hyun Kim and Yesola Kweon 2026

ISBNs: 9781009461054 (HB), 9781009461047 (PB), 9781009461030 (OC)
ISSNs: 2753-8117 (online), 2753-8109 (print)

Contents

1 Political Attitudes and the Intersections of Marginalized Identities — 1

2 Descriptive Representation of Class and Gender: Measurement and Empirical Patterns — 6

3 The Class- and Gender-Based Divisions in Policy Priorities — 19

4 How Class and Gender Interact to Shape Political Attitudes — 41

5 Conclusion — 57

References — 61

An Online Appendix is available at www.Cambridge.org/Kim/Kweon

1 Political Attitudes and the Intersections of Marginalized Identities

In September 2017, the *New York Times* featured an article examining the perceptions of female German citizens regarding the impact of Chancellor Angela Merkel's leadership, marking her as one of the world's longest-serving female national leaders.[1] Merkel, elected in 2005, held office for 16 years, a duration that challenged conventional perceptions of political leadership, traditionally associated with men. Interestingly, despite Merkel's tenure, interviews showcased in the article suggested that her leadership did not necessarily enhance the lives and status of women. This gap between symbolic representation and material advancement raises important questions about the limits of elite female leadership in addressing the needs of more socioeconomically vulnerable women. Merkel herself holds a PhD in physics and comes from a professional, highly educated background – traits that place her far from the working-class women most affected by economic insecurity, occupational segregation, and gendered precarity.

According to World Bank data, in Germany, as of 2024, where 46.5% of the workforce comprises women, with a proportion similar to men possessing university degrees, there persists a disparity. Approximately 59% of women in the workforce engage in part-time jobs, often involuntarily, contributing to a substantial pay gap (18% as of 2023), exceeding the OECD average. This issue isn't exclusive to Germany but is prevalent in many democracies.[2] This issue extends beyond Germany and is prevalent in numerous democracies worldwide. It underscores that merely increasing female participation in politics may not guarantee improved representation across all societal sectors. This is particularly evident when significant class-based disparities influence women's political preferences. This prompts the question: How do class and gender intersect in shaping individuals' policy preferences and political attitudes? In addressing this inquiry, the Element delves into the nuanced perspective that class experiences are inherently gendered, highlighting the intricate ways in which socioeconomic status intersects with gender identities. While economic class undoubtedly plays a significant role in socialization and political inclination formation, its impact varies distinctly between genders.

For men, economic class often shapes perceptions of authority, stability, and the provider role, thereby influencing their political preferences toward policies that protect or enhance their economic standing. In contrast, women's political attitudes are shaped by the intersection of class and gender, producing more

---

[1] See www.nytimes.com/2017/09/13/world/europe/angela-merkel-germany-election.html.
[2] See www.dw.com/en/gender-pay-gap-in-germany-women-earn-18-less-than-men/a-68022521.

complex patterns across socioeconomic groups. The greater financial vulnerability of working-class women – due to their concentration in low-wage, insecure, and gender-segregated occupations, for instance – may heighten their support for social welfare, family policies, and gender equality initiatives relative to white-collar women. This tendency may be further amplified in countries with larger gender wage gaps, where economic inequalities disproportionately burden working-class women.

Hence, this Element emphasizes the necessity of recognizing the complex interplay between class and gender in shaping political attitudes and policy preferences. It advocates for a nuanced understanding that transcends simplistic categorizations, shedding light on how gendered experiences intersect with socioeconomic status to shape the political landscape. By unpacking these complexities, this Element aims to contribute to a more inclusive and insightful discourse on citizens' political beliefs and policy advocacy.

Prior to elaborating and testing our arguments, this introductory section provides a succinct overview of how current research on gender and politics adopts an intersectional approach to marginalized identities. Expanding on these studies, we delve into the significance of recognizing the interconnectedness of gender and class in comprehending women's political attitudes.

1.1 Studies of the Intersectionality of Marginalized Identities

Within the realm of political science research, scholars are increasingly highlighting the paramount importance of acknowledging the intersectional nature of identities (Cohen, 2009; Gershon et al., 2019; Hancock, 2007). This perspective posits that the conventional "single-dimension" approach, which focuses solely on one aspect of identity, offers only a partial understanding of the sociopolitical experiences of marginalized groups. Instead, proponents argue that a comprehensive understanding necessitates recognition of the intricate and intersecting nature of various social identities. A growing body of literature has emphasized the intersectional dynamics between gender and race and ethnicity and their significant implications for a range of political outcomes (Bejarano et al., 2011; Gay and Tate, 1998; Gershon et al., 2019; Liu et al. 2025; Philpot and Walton Jr., 2007; Simien and Clawson, 2004; Smooth, 2011). Notably, much of this scholarship on intersectionality in gender and politics has emerged from studies of the political experiences and behavior of Black women – and more recently, Latina voters – laying a critical foundation for extending intersectional analysis to other groups with multiple marginalized identities.

In the realm of political science research, there has been a long-standing tradition that suggests shared experiences among members of marginalized groups, rooted in their group affiliations, foster a sense of collective identity and solidarity, thereby promoting collective political action. Scholarship in minority politics underscores the significance of linked fate – a belief that group members encounter shared challenges, shaped by a collective history of group-based marginalization (Dawson, 1995; Tate, 1994). A pivotal finding within this body of research is the pronounced tendency for voters from ethnoracial minority backgrounds to rally behind candidates of their own ethnic or racial group (Barreto, 2010; McDermott, 1998). However, this approach often operates under the assumption that members of a particular social group share homogenous experiences, often overlooking the diversity inherent within the group (Hancock, 2007).

In recent decades, an increasing number of scholars have engaged in discussions surrounding the intersectionality of multiple identities within political experiences, challenging the assumption of uniformity within marginalized groups. This approach rejects the notion that members of marginalized groups, such as women or ethnoracial minorities, universally share identical experiences within their respective groups. Instead, it recognizes the presence of sociopolitical stratification among subgroups within these larger groups, resulting in distinct experiences for different subcategories. Black feminist scholars, most notably Crenshaw (1989, 1991), have coined the term "intersectionality" to describe this interplay of multiple identities, particularly gender and race, which they argue creates compounded discrimination against black women. They contend that focusing solely on one dimension of identity, such as gender or race, fails to capture the unique struggles faced by Black women (Brah and Phoenix, 2004; C. Cohen, 2009; Hancock, 2007), advocating instead for research that considers the intersections of multiple marginalizations.

Drawing from this theoretical framework, political scientists have empirically investigated how the intersectionality of gender and race influences the political attitudes and behavior of women of color. Research demonstrates that the racial and gender identities of women of color mutually shape their perceptions of political events and policy attitudes (Bejarano et al., 2011; Gay and Tate, 1998; Simien and Clawson, 2004). For example, Black women or Latinas exhibit stronger support for gender equality compared to Black men or Latinos (Bejarano et al., 2011; Simien and Clawson, 2004).

Scholars have also explored how the interplay of racial and gender identity influences the candidate evaluation and voting behavior of women of color, particularly focusing on the role of intersectional minority linked fate (Gershon et al., 2019). Notably, Philpot and Walton Jr. (2007) found that Black women are the demographic group most likely to support Black female candidates, possibly due to gender differences in perceptions of representation among ethnoracial minority voters. Black women or Latina voters are more inclined to view a candidate as representing their interests when they share racial and gender identities with the candidate (Bejarano et al., 2021; Gershon et al., 2019).

While some scholars, like McCall (2002), advocate for the broader application of intersectionality beyond gender and race, few studies have examined the intersection of gender and class. Despite substantial scholarly attention dedicated to exploring gender disparities in political engagement, the influence of socioeconomic status, particularly class, remains a critical yet often overlooked factor. This Element underscores the importance of understanding the intersection of gender and class in unraveling the complexities of women's political attitudes and behaviors. So why does class matter in understanding women's political attitudes?

1.2 Why Class Matters in Understanding Women's Political Attitudes

Across most democratic nations, the working class finds itself severely underrepresented in political spheres, a disparity underscored in Section 2 of our study. Politicians, particularly those on the national stage, predominantly hail from privileged backgrounds, boasting professional careers and higher educational attainments (Barnes et al., 2021; Carnes, 2012; O'Grady, 2019). This glaring discrepancy becomes even more pronounced when focusing solely on female representation. Barnes et al. (2021) reveal that even at the state legislature level in the United States, the proportion of working-class politicians remains below 10%. This proportion diminishes further to less than 1% when examining exclusively female representatives. Indeed, numerous studies indicate that the majority of women holding office typically possess robust professional backgrounds and academic achievements (Anzia and Berry, 2011; Lazarus and Steigerwalt, 2018; Volden et al., 2013). Nevertheless, across most advanced democracies, despite recent advancements in women's education and employment, a substantial portion of women find themselves employed in precarious or low-paying positions, perpetuating a persistent wage gap.

Globally, women's workforce participation faces formidable challenges due to occupational segregation, wage disparities, and economic vulnerability, particularly concentrated in blue-collar and pink-collar occupations (O'Connor, 1993; Hoque and Kirkpatrick, 2003). Such disparities are compounded by gendered societal norms and expectations, which often limit women's access to higher-paying or traditionally male-dominated industries.

Class emerges as a crucial moderating factor in shaping the impact of political representation on public attitudes (Barnes and Saxton, 2019; Carnes,

2012; Carnes and Lupu, 2016). However, while class representation influences the political behavior of all voters, class dynamics intersect with gender, yielding distinctive effects on women's political beliefs and behaviors. As expounded in Section 3, working-class women often prioritize issues such as health care access, wage equality, and family support programs, reflecting their experiences of economic insecurity, resource constraints, and struggles for financial stability. Conversely, white-collar women, buoyed by relative economic stability and career aspirations, may place greater emphasis on concerns such as corporate governance, work–life balance, and education reform.

Beyond shaping policy preferences, class also influences women's perceptions of politics and political efficacy. Economic precarity tends to erode individuals' trust and confidence in government, fostering a sense of disconnect and alienation from political processes (Barnes and Saxton, 2019; Chi et al., 2013; Norris, 2015; Schraff, 2017). Given the disproportionate impact of economic insecurity on women, owing to their overrepresentation in low-paid precarious jobs, the political repercussions of such insecurity are particularly pronounced among females. Moreover, considering the significant disparity between women's representation in the workforce and in politics, the class-related effects of representation exert a substantial influence on female voters (Kweon, 2024). This disparity underscores systemic barriers that hinder working-class women's access to political power and influence, perpetuating cycles of underrepresentation and marginalization.

Consequently, as outlined in Section 4, working-class women often harbor feelings of distrust and skepticism toward the political system. They frequently perceive mainstream political discourse as detached and irrelevant to their daily lives, fostering a sense of political disengagement. In contrast, white-collar women, endowed with access to resources, networks, and educational opportunities, exhibit higher levels of political efficacy and engagement. They are more inclined to participate in various political activities, such as voting, volunteering, and advocacy, viewing themselves as capable of influencing political outcomes and effecting change within the system.

By illuminating the distinct policy preferences and political attitudes of working-class versus white-collar women, this study yields profound implications for democratic representation and political engagement. It underscores how economic precarity exacerbates distrust and alienation from the political system, particularly among working-class women, while underscoring the disproportionate impact of class representation on female voters. By shedding light on these dynamics, the study contributes to a deeper understanding of the barriers to political participation faced by working-class women, emphasizing the imperative of recognizing the nuanced differences in the political attitudes and experiences of women across different class backgrounds for the development of more inclusive and effective policies.

1.3 Roadmap of the Element

The following sections of this Element investigate how class and gender jointly shape political attitudes, policy preferences, and political behavior. Section 2 presents empirical evidence of the severe underrepresentation of working-class women in politics and identifies the structural barriers that sustain this imbalance. Section 3 elaborates our theoretical framework and analyzes cross-national data to demonstrate how gendered class experiences produce divergent policy priorities among women. Section 4 shifts the focus to political behavior and attitudes, examining how economic insecurity shapes political efficacy, democratic satisfaction, and voting behavior – particularly support for radical right parties and tendencies toward political disengagement – across different class backgrounds. Section 5 discusses the broader implications of these findings for democratic representation and policy responsiveness, offering concrete recommendations for building more inclusive political systems. Taken together, these sections challenge the assumption of women as a politically unified group and underscore the importance of attending to class-based divisions in shaping women's political lives.

2 Descriptive Representation of Class and Gender: Measurement and Empirical Patterns

Existing research has amply demonstrated how a group's descriptive representation is linked to a variety of its members' political attitudes, including a sense of political inclusion, political efficacy, or trust in government (Atkeson and Carrillo, 2007; Barnes and Burchard, 2013; Barnes and Saxton, 2019; Mansbridge, 1999). Given the centrality of descriptive representation in the formation of political attitudes, we first need to examine patterns of class and gender representation before exploring how individuals' class and gender backgrounds intersect to shape their political preferences and attitudes.

In this section, we examine recent and historical empirical trends in class and gender representation in advanced democracies. The section focuses on the descriptive representation of class and gender. First, we review existing research on class representation to identify empirical strategies for conceptualizing and measuring the descriptive representation of working-class individuals. Specifically, we develop strategies for classifying politicians' class backgrounds into white-collar, blue-collar, and pink-collar. We then illustrate the patterns of class and gender representation in national legislatures using the case of the United States and the United Kingdom. Finally, we draw conclusions and discuss the implications of our analysis for the study of class and gender representation.

2.1 Measuring Descriptive Representation of the Working Class

How do we measure the extent to which the working class is represented in political bodies? With a growing academic consensus on the importance of representing diverse social classes (see, for example, Barnes et al., 2023; Carnes, 2013; Carnes and Lupu, 2015; Elsässer and Schäfer, 2022; Grumbach, 2015), scholars have proposed several different ways to conceptualize and measure descriptive representation of the working class. A dominant approach in previous research has been to focus on representatives' occupational backgrounds. In this approach, the class background of politicians is categorized based on their occupations prior to entering politics. For example, Carnes (2013) defines working-class politicians as those who previously worked as manual laborers, service workers, or union officials. O'Grady (2019) uses a similar approach when coding the class backgrounds of legislators in the British Parliament. In his work, legislators who worked as manual or manufacturing workers, those who worked in unskilled jobs in the service sector, or those who worked full-time for a union representing manual workers are considered working class. Others suggest using more fine-grained measures by looking at other components of social class, such as education and income. According to this view, there is a hierarchy within individuals in the same occupation based on their level of education or social mobility (Oesch, 2006). For example, some scholars argue for a distinction between the routine working class and the skilled working class, which is wealthier and better educated than the former (Wüest and Pontusson, 2022). Following this approach, retail salespersons selling luxury goods are not considered as belonging to the same class as cashiers in a local supermarket. This classification takes into account varying education/skill levels within similar occupations, rather than grouping all retail workers as working-class individuals.

In addition, an emerging body of work focuses on gender differences in employment across industries and their implications for representation. While earlier research relied on the white-collar/working-class distinction, recent studies emphasize the importance of considering occupational gender segregation in conceptualizing class representation (Barnes et al., 2021; Betz et al., 2023; Murray, 2023). In particular, these studies propose expanding the concept of working-class representation to include the representation of pink-collar

Table 1 Measures of class background in each section

	Measure of class background	Classification
Section 2	Occupation	White-Collar/Blue-Collar/Pink-Collar
Section 3 3.4	Occupation	White-Collar/Blue-Collar/Pink-Collar
3.5	Occupational Skill	White-Collar (High-Skilled)/Working-Class (Low-Skilled)
Section 4	Occupational Skill	White-Collar (High-Skilled)/Working-Class (Low-Skilled)

occupations. Pink-collar occupations refer to low-status, low-skill occupations that are predominantly held by women (Barnes et al., 2021). These occupations typically include clerical and secretarial jobs, as well as nonprofessional jobs in social services or personal care. Under this classification method, manual workers, such as factory workers or railway workers, will be classified distinctly from low-skilled service workers, such as care workers or call-center workers, rather than being grouped into a single category of the working-class. Individuals with pink-collar backgrounds have occupational experiences and socialization that substantially differ from those in traditional blue-collar jobs, such as manual laborers, which in turn lead them to develop unique policy preferences. For instance, pink-collar occupations typically have significantly lower unionization rates, less job security, and fewer employment benefits compared to blue-collar jobs (Jokela, 2019; Kalleberg, 2012). Differentiating between politicians with pink-collar backgrounds and those with blue-collar backgrounds, while considering both as working class, allows us to better reflect these differences.

Throughout this Element, we employ different measurements for individuals' class backgrounds. In this section, we analyze patterns of class representation by gender using fine-grained, occupation-based measurements of representatives' class backgrounds. In later sections, due to data availability constraints, we use occupational skill levels as a proxy measure for class backgrounds. Table 1 summarizes the different measures used in each section.

2.2 Patterns of Class and Gender Representation

To examine patterns of class and gender representation, we choose two democracies as our case: the United States and the United Kingdom. These two countries represent established democracies with a relatively long history and a high degree of institutional stability. We combine existing approaches to conceptualizing class and gender representation in the following ways. First, we measure the descriptive representation of each socioeconomic class based on the numerical presence of legislators who share their professional experience. Second, we depart from the classic working-class/white-collar dichotomy in classifying one's class background to incorporate gender segregation in occupation by adding a category of pink-collar workers.

Figure 1 shows the occupational breakdown of legislators in our data, disaggregated by gender (US: top panel, UK: bottom panel). In both countries, the gender gap among white-collar legislators has narrowed in recent years. In contrast, the number of women from blue-collar and pink-collar backgrounds has remained abysmally low, even in recent years. In the following sections, we provide more detailed information about these patterns.

2.2.1 US House of Representatives

We begin by examining class representation in the US House of Representatives. Of the two chambers of the US Congress that make policies of national importance, we focus on the House because its members tend to be

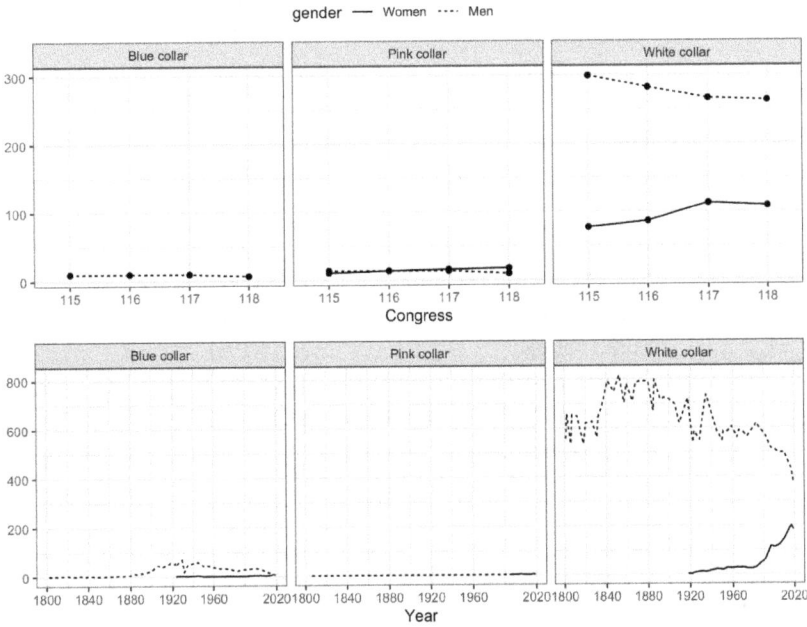

Figure 1 Gender makeup of legislators with different class backgrounds; top panel: US Congress; bottom panel: UK Parliament

relatively more diverse than the Senate, which is composed of more homogeneous members in terms of economic background (Carnes, 2012). We collected demographic and occupational information on 702 representatives who have ever served in the House of Representatives from the 115th to the 118th Congresses (from January 3, 2017, to January 3, 2025). In addition to representatives who were originally elected to office at the beginning of the term, our sample also includes those who filled vacancies between elections. Analyzing the class backgrounds of House members over this period allows us to examine whether individuals from different class backgrounds are represented in legislative decision-making at the national level, and how the extent of class representation has changed over time. In Table 2, we report the demographic

Table 2 Demographic characteristics of the US sample

Characteristic	$N = 702$
Gender	
Women	188 (27%)
Men	514 (73%)
Party	
Democrat	322 (46%)
Republican	377 (54%)
Independent	3 (0.4%)
Age	
Range	23–91
Mean (SD)	56.66 (12.58)
NA	2
Education	
Lower than high school	1 (0.1%)
High school	6 (0.9%)
Some college	22 (3.1%)
College graduate	228 (33%)
Vocational/Technical school	2 (0.3%)
Postgraduate degree	442 (63%)
NA	1
Race	
Asian	18 (2.6%)
Black	80 (11%)
Latino	55 (7.8%)
White	549 (78%)

characteristics, including gender, age, and educational attainment, and the partisan breakdown of the House members included in our sample. Perhaps not surprisingly, the vast majority of House members are men and highly educated. Less than 30% of our sample are female legislators, and only about 5% of our sample have less than a college education. Also, white legislators make up the vast majority of the sample.

Following the dominant approach in the literature, we operationalize the class backgrounds of House members based on their former occupations. Specifically, we categorize their class backgrounds as (1) white-collar, (2) blue-collar, and (3) pink-collar. Instead of a white-collar/working-class dichotomy, we distinguish between blue-collar and pink-collar workers, although we consider both groups to be working class. We believe that the distinction between blue-collar and pink-collar backgrounds is crucial given the persistence of gender segregation in occupations and the unique socialization and occupational experiences of individuals who belong to each group (Barnes et al., 2021, Murray, 2023). It is particularly relevant for the purposes of our research, as we are interested in the intersectional nature of class and gender representation. Following the coding schemes of Carnes (2012, 2013), we classify businessmen, private sector professionals, lawyers, and politicians as individuals with white-collar backgrounds, and manual workers and union members as blue-collar backgrounds. Next, following the coding scheme introduced in Barnes, Beall, and Holman (2021), we classify legislators as having a pink-collar background if they previously worked in service-oriented occupations that are predominantly held by women, such as teachers, social workers, and caregivers. Table 3 provides a list of all occupations in our sample by class background. Note that a sizable subset of legislators ($N = 62$) had occupations that did not fall into any of the three categories, such as army officers, police officers, and firefighters.

Using this information on legislators' backgrounds, we infer patterns of class and gender representation in the US House of Representatives. Figure 2 illustrates how the composition of legislators' class backgrounds varies over time and by gender. The most striking pattern in the figure is the contrast between the large proportion of white-collar legislators and the small proportion of blue- and pink-collar legislators: In the 115th Congress, only 10 of the 448 House members had blue-collar backgrounds, and 25 of them had pink-collar occupations. In contrast, about 84% of the legislators had white-collar backgrounds. As shown in Figure 2, the number of working-class (either blue-collar or pink-collar) legislators has increased over time, but not by much. Overall, this pattern is consistent with previous research on this topic using data from earlier sessions of Congress (Carnes, 2012).

Table 3 List of occupations by class backgrounds in the US House of Representatives

White-Collar (N = 586)	Blue-Collar (N = 12)	Pink-Collar (N = 42)	Others/NA (N = 62)
Businesspeople (Agriculture, Finance, Insurance, Investment, Real estate, Intelligence, Transportation, Contractor, etc.), Lawyer, Judge, Doctor, Dentist, Pharmacist, Journalist, Policy advisor, Politician, Diplomat, Accountant, Journalist, Real estate agent, Public servant, CIA officer, Academic, Urban planner, Political consultant, Sports agent, Prosecutor, Public relations, Pilot, Engineer	Farmer, Union worker, Taxi driver, Machinist, Automotive worker, Carpenter, Manufacturing plant worker	Teacher, Social worker, 911 dispatcher, Nurse, Educator, Social service administrator, Customer service, Care practitioner, Insurance agent, Administrator, Wellness coordinator, Sales, Operator	Army, Navy, Marine, Police Officer, Detective, Firefighter, Athlete

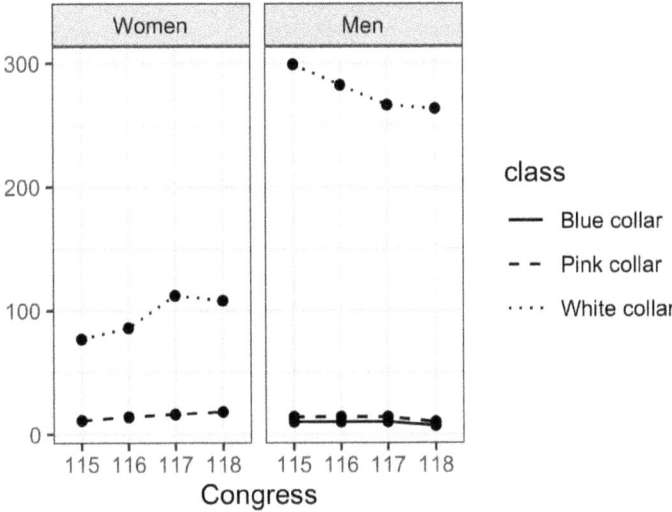

Figure 2 Patterns of class representation in the 115th–118th US Congress by gender

Notably, Figure 2 also suggests important gender patterns in class representation. The left panel of Figure 2 shows that none of the female House members in our sample held blue-collar occupations, and all of the women legislators with working-class backgrounds held pink-collar occupations. This pattern highlights the importance of disaggregating working-class occupations into blue-collar and pink-collar occupations in order to fully assess how legislators represent the diverse experiences and preferences that may exist within the working-class population (Barnes et al., 2021). In addition, of the 188 women legislators in our sample, only 14% had pink-collar jobs, while the vast majority (81%) had white-collar backgrounds. The right panel suggests that there are some men legislators who previously held pink-collar jobs, which is explained by the large number of male teachers in our sample. Most importantly, Figure 2 suggests that working-class women have the smallest numerical presence in Congress, followed by working men, white-collar women, and white-collar men.

To examine potential partisan differences in class representation, we disaggregate the data by legislators' party affiliation. Figure 3 illustrates the changes in the number of House members with different class backgrounds from the 115th to the 118th Congress, disaggregated by gender and party affiliation. The figure shows a partisan gap in working-class representation, particularly among male legislators. The proportion of Republican male legislators with blue-collar or white-collar backgrounds is about twice that of Democratic male legislators. The difference in proportion is statistically significant at the conventional level

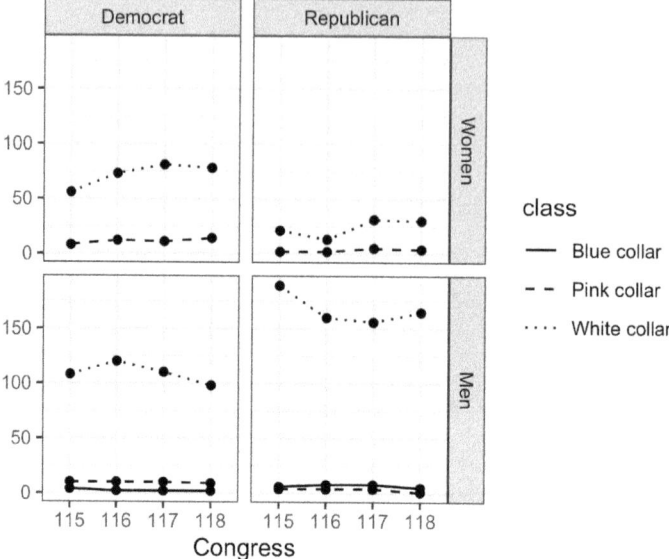

Figure 3 Class representation by gender and party

(chi-squared test, *p*-value: 0.058). The partisan difference in the proportion of working-class legislators is not clearly visible among female legislators. The share of female legislators with working-class occupations is 13% in the Republican Party and 14% in the Democratic Party.

2.2.2 UK Sample

In addition to the US Congress, we examine the gender and class composition of legislators in the British Parliament. Compared to the United States, British parties tend to have stronger class affiliations, with the Labour Party traditionally representing the working class and the Conservative Party representing the upper class. This feature in the UK allows us to examine how class and gender representations might vary according to the party's attachment to working-class voters. For the British legislator data, we use the Comparative Legislators (Göbel and Munzert, 2022), which provides legislator data for 16 countries. For the United Kingdom, the data includes information on 11,321 legislators for all 58 parliamentary sessions from 1801 to 2019. The long time span of the data allows us to examine how the class and gender composition of legislators in the British Parliament has changed over time. The data includes politicians' names, political party, occupational background, gender, ethnicity, religion, and year of birth and death. This information is compiled by integrating data from Wikipedia, Wikidata, and other sources. Based on the occupational information, we coded politicians' class backgrounds into four categories, as shown in Table 4: white-collar, blue-collar, pink-collar, and

Table 4 List of occupations by class backgrounds in the UK Parliament

White-Collar (N = 10,712)	Blue-Collar (N = 341)	Pink-Collar (N = 16)	Others/NA (N = 74)
Accountant, Alderman, Art collector, Banker, Barrister, Biographer, Business executive, Dentist, Diplomat, Financier, Fund manager, Investment banker, Consultant, Landowner, Fil maker, Politician, Government official, Surgeon, Pharmacist, Physician, Journalist, Urban planner, etc.	Blacksmith, Carpenter, Coal miner, Electrician, Farmer, Glassmaker, Horticulturist, Ocean rower, Railway worker, Sailor, Shipbuilder, Trade unionist, Union organizer, Weaver	Teacher, Nurse, Librarian, Social worker, Steward, Clerk, Trainer	Animal rights advocate, Athlete, Military personnel, Explorer, Actor, Philatelist, Socialite, Racing automobile driver, Sculptor, Radio personality, Photographer, Peace activist, Painter, Musician

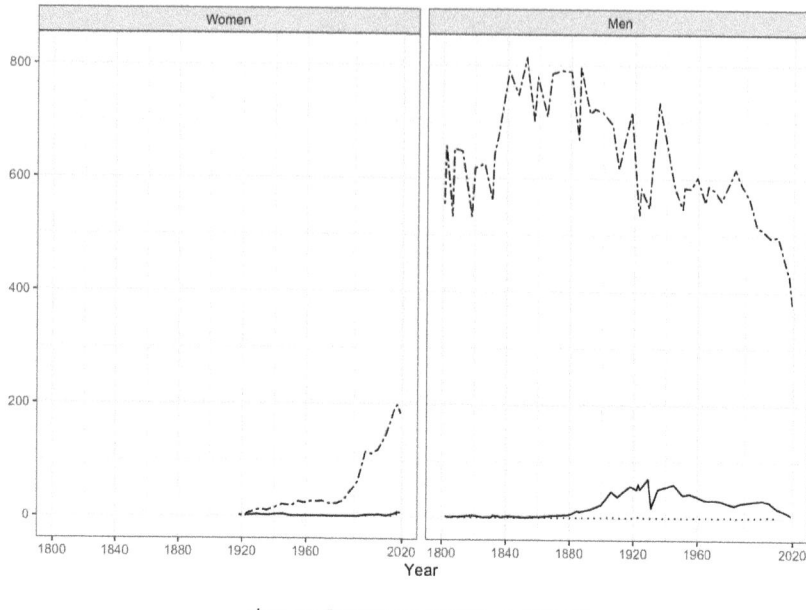

Figure 4 Class representation in UK Parliament by MPs' gender (1801–2019)

other. For some politicians, the data provide multiple previous occupations. In this case, if a politician previously held at least one pink-collar or blue-collar occupation, we categorized the person as having a pink-collar or blue-collar occupational background.

Figure 4 shows historical trends in class representation in the British Parliament from 1800 to 2019. Overall, we see similar patterns of class representation in our British parliamentary data to those in the United States, although the underrepresentation of working-class backgrounds is even more profound in the UK. Over the two hundred years in our sample, MPs from white-collar backgrounds have consistently made up an overwhelming majority of the British Parliament, while those from working-class backgrounds (blue-collar and pink-collar combined) make up a tiny proportion, ranging from 0.23% to 12% of all MPs. Figure 4 also shows the severe underrepresentation of women, especially working-class women, in the British Parliament. Although the number of women MPs has gradually increased over time since they were first elected to Parliament in 1919, the left panel of Figure 4 suggests that the increase in white-collar women alone accounts for the increased presence of women in Parliament. While British women have gained numerical representation in the national legislature over time, albeit marginally, this

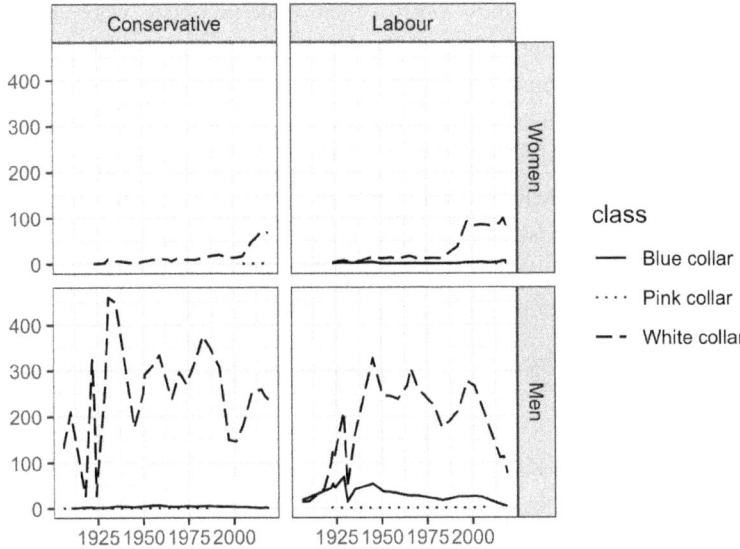

Figure 5 Class representation in the UK Parliament by gender and party

pattern reveals that there is still a glaring representation gap where legislators who share the lived experiences of working-class women are almost invisible.

Compared to their counterparts in the United States, the major political parties in the United Kingdom have historically maintained closer ties to social groups divided along economic class lines. In particular, the British Labour Party has developed a reputation for representing working-class voters, although this reputation has weakened in recent decades as the party has moved to the center-right (Evans and Tilley, 2017; Heath, 2018). Given the relatively prominent role of class cleavage in the United Kingdom, we may observe different patterns of class representation across parties. We therefore conduct a party-level comparison of class representation, focusing on the two main governing parties: Conservatives and Labour. We limit the time frame to after 1900, when the Labor Party became a major political party in government.

Figure 5 displays the comparison of class representation between the Conservative and Labour parties. The bottom panels of Figure 5 suggest some meaningful partisan differences in class representation among men MPs. While working-class MPs make up a very small proportion of all male MPs in both parties, there have been far more blue-collar men MPs in the Labour Party than in the Conservative Party. Partisan difference in working-class representation is weaker among women MPs, as shown in the top panels. Both the Conservative and Labour parties have had very few working-class women MPs throughout the period of our study. In the Labour Party, a small number of women MPs from blue-collar backgrounds, most of them trade unionists, were elected to Parliament. It was not until 1997 that the party began electing a small number of women MPs who had pink-collar jobs, such as nurses and social workers. In the Conservative Party, there was only one woman MP with a pink-collar background –Anne Milton, who had worked as a nurse before her parliamentary career, and no woman MP from a blue-collar background. Our party comparison suggests that even those political parties with closer ties to working-class voters, such as the British Labour Party, fail to represent voters from different class backgrounds, and this pattern is more profound among women voters.

2.3 Summary and Implications

Using demographic and occupational information on legislators in the United States and the United Kingdom, this section examined patterns of class and gender representation in national legislatures. While the underrepresentation of working-class voters is well documented in existing research (Barnes and Saxton, 2019; Carnes, 2013, 2012; Heath, 2018), we believe our intersectional approach offers deeper insights into the challenges of democratic representation. Specifically, our analysis in the two advanced democracies reveals several common gendered patterns in class representation. First, and most importantly, there is a severe shortage of female legislators from working-class backgrounds in both countries. The overwhelming majority of national legislatures in these countries consist of legislators from elite backgrounds, and the working-class legislators who make up a small fraction of the total are mostly men. Although women's descriptive representation has increased over time in both countries, working-class women are still largely absent from their national legislatures.

The second point concerns partisan differences in class representation. While our analysis shows that there are more male working-class legislators from left-leaning parties, such as the Democratic Party in the United States or the British Labour Party, this partisan difference is weaker or nonexistent when it comes to female legislators. This pattern suggests that working-class women are marginalized by political parties across the aisle. This representation gap has crucial implications for the political attitudes of working-class women voters. As we will show in the following section, working-class women have distinct policy priorities and preferences that differ significantly from those of working-class men or white-collar women. Thus, we expect that the exclusion from formal politics of lawmakers who share their unique lived experiences and understand their policy priorities will have a crucial impact on how working-class women voters view politics.

3 The Class- and Gender-Based Divisions in Policy Priorities

In this section, we provide a theoretical framework and empirical test for the class-based divisions in women's policy priorities across and within policy areas. While existing research tends to focus on identifying differences in policy preferences across social groups, understanding the policy priorities of the masses is just as important as studying their policy preferences because they closely reflect individuals' interests, values, or the issues that are most relevant to their everyday lives. This section examines how the types of policies prioritized by working-class women differ from those considered most important by other groups, particularly white-collar women. While previous research often conceptualizes women as a single bloc with homogeneous political preferences, we argue that this conventional approach fails to fully capture the important differences in women's policy priorities that emerge along their class backgrounds.

We first review the prior research on gender and class-based differences in policy priorities and argue for the importance of class-based heterogeneity in policy priorities that can emerge within the same gender group. We then discuss our theoretical expectations about how class background might influence women's policy priorities. Specifically, building on insights from political economy research on gender segregations in occupations, we expect that the financial vulnerability experienced by working-class women will lead them to prioritize social welfare issues, family policies, and gender equality issues more than any other class-gender group. We further expect this tendency to be stronger in countries with larger gender wage gaps, as these inequalities disproportionately affect working-class women.

We empirically examine class-based divisions using (1) original surveys that are conducted in the United States and the UK and (2) the Comparative Study of Electoral System datasets, which pool post-election surveys from over 30 countries since 1996. We use Module 3 of the dataset, which includes a unique set of questions measuring respondents' political priorities and preferred policy positions.

3.1 Gender and Class-Based Differences in Policy Preference and Priorities

A large body of research has documented gender differences in policy preferences. Studies have shown that women are more likely than men to support redistribution and the expansion of social welfare programs (Funk and Gathmann, 2015; Lizotte, 2022; Lizotte and Carey Jr., 2021). These different policy preferences often translate into gender differences in voting behavior, with women voters more likely than men to vote for a left-wing party (Box-Steffensmeier et al., 2004; Kittilson, 2016). Research suggests that gender differences in political preferences may arise from different psychological tendencies between men and women. This line of work finds that women are less risk-taking and more pro-social than men (Andreoni and Vesterlund, 2001; Niederle and Vesterlund, 2007). Other studies reveal that women tend to hold more egalitarian views and thus are more supportive of government policies designed to help the poor (Barnes and Cassese, 2017; Huddy et al., 2008), which may explain their stronger preference for expanded government social welfare programs and spending.

Given gender differences in social roles and experiences of socialization processes, we may observe substantial variations in the policy areas men and women prioritize. Previous research on gender differences in policy priorities has focused on the differential legislative priorities of male and female legislators. This line of research aims to investigate the relationship between women's descriptive and substantive representation and has demonstrated gender differences in legislative priorities. For instance, studies have shown that female legislators are more likely to prioritize "women's issues" than their male counterparts in their legislative activities, including bill sponsorship and floor speeches (Atkinson and Windett, 2019; Dietrich et al., 2019; Lawless, 2015; Schwindt-Bayer, 2010). Yildirim (2022) highlights the importance of studying women's interests at the mass level for a more rigorous assessment of substantive representation. While this study finds that women are more likely than men to prioritize women's issues such as education, health policy, and welfare, there is considerable heterogeneity in policy priorities across partisan or racial groups. This finding underscores the need to move away from the scholarly tradition that views women as a homogeneous political bloc and instead examine how different subgroups of women formulate their policy priorities.

Research shows that social class background has a crucial influence on individuals' policy attitudes and their prioritization of different policy areas. Class and occupational backgrounds shape both material interests and potential benefits from specific policy programs (Fernández and Jaime-Castillo, 2018; Kitschelt and Rehm, 2014). Moreover, class profoundly affects lived experiences, socialization processes, and broader worldviews (Lee, 2023; Lott, 2002; Manza and Brooks, 2008). Previous research on this topic has extensively examined how social class shapes attitudes toward redistributive policies. Empirical studies have found working-class individuals tend to favor increased levels of income redistribution, compared to people with white-collar individuals (Kitschelt and Rehm, 2014; Svallfors, 2006). Scholars explain this tendency among working-class people with various factors including skill specificity, employment conditions, and economic mobility. Notably, research shows that workers in working-class occupations often possess specialized skills that limit job mobility, making them particularly vulnerable to job loss and economic uncertainty (Iversen and Soskice, 2001; Rehm, 2009). This occupational constraint helps explain why they tend to place high priority on income redistribution and social welfare policies as protection against financial instability and risks. While this research provides valuable insights into how social class shapes policy attitudes, it has not adequately examined gender differences in social and economic experiences within classes. Understanding these differences is crucial, as they may lead to distinct policy priorities between working-class men and women. Consequently, politicians' understanding of working-class policy interests may overlook the unique priorities of working-class women.

3.2 Theory and Hypotheses

In this section, we examine whether and how women from different class backgrounds prioritize different policy issues, focusing on class-based differences in their emphasis on social welfare and gender equality issues. We theorize that the increased financial vulnerability of working-class women leads them to place greater importance on social welfare policies than women with higher socioeconomic status. We further expect that greater wage inequality between men and women reinforces this tendency.

Research has shown that women tend to prioritize social welfare issues over military or economic issues (Andersen, 1999; Inglehart and Norris, 2003). A central explanation for this finding focuses on the gender division of household labor. Women tend to take on more responsibility for housework and childcare than men. Their responsibilities as mothers or caregivers for the elderly increase women's policy needs for social programs that can compensate for the unique risks associated with these responsibilities (Estévez-Abe, 2006). For example, in addition to employment security programs such as unemployment insurance or pensions, women place priority on family policies that include maternity leave and childcare.

At the same time, whether an individual prioritizes social welfare over other policy issues depends heavily on his or her financial vulnerability and, by extension, economic class. There are reasons to believe that working-class women are particularly vulnerable to financial insecurity and thus have greater demands for social welfare programs than any other class-gender groups. While class differences in wages and job security are not specific to women, the political economy literature suggests that class-based wage inequalities may be more pronounced for women than for men because of the concentration of working-class women in industries or occupations with low wages and job insecurity.

A large body of work has demonstrated the persistence of gender segregation in occupations where working-class women are overrepresented in the service sector, such as personal care, cleaning, health care, or sales (Goldin, 1994; Polachek, 1981; Tomaskovic-Devey et al., 2006). In addition, women are disproportionately employed in clerical or secretarial jobs in the industry, while men are more likely to hold managerial positions. These jobs that predominantly employ women, known as "pink-collar" occupations, typically pay less than working-class jobs dominated by men. Research suggests that this wage disparity exists because society places less value on work and abilities traditionally associated with women, such as caregiving and community service (Charles and Grusky, 2005). Moreover, pink-collar jobs in the service sector typically have a high proportion of nonstandard employment contracts, such as temporary or fixed-term contracts, resulting in low job security for workers. Consequently, many female-dominated working-class jobs, such as care work, are classified as "precarious work," where workers have little control over the duration of their jobs and lack collective bargaining power (Jokela, 2019; Kalleberg, 2012). Policies aimed at reducing the gender pay gap tend to focus on high-status elite jobs, leaving behind women in working-class jobs (Mandel and Shalev, 2009; McCall, 2002). While policies to reduce gender gaps in pay and employment, such as equal pay or parental leave, apply only to full-time workers, a large proportion of working-class women's jobs are part-time, depriving these women of access to equality policies. Recent research suggests that occupational gender segregation even reinforces women's underrepresentation in politics, as individuals with feminine occupations are less likely to develop political ambition and seek high-profile political offices (Bernhard and Holman, 2025). It also has broader implications for public opinion on gender relations, as it reinforces stereotypes about gender roles in society (Jung and Tavits, 2024). In sum, gender segregation in occupations has created self-reinforcing patterns of inequality, where working-class women tend to have jobs that pay less and offer less security than those held by working-class men.

While women have made significant advancements into formerly male-dominated professional fields like law, medicine, and management, there has been much less progress in integrating women into blue-collar work. Why do we see the persistence of gender segregation in occupations despite its detrimental effect on gender equality? Research notes that in working-class occupations, there remains a strong belief that men and women have fundamentally different abilities and natural skillsets (England, 2010). This widespread gender essentialism deters women from crossing gender lines to pursue male-dominated blue-collar positions, despite these jobs offering better pay, security, and employment benefits. Research suggests that women are more likely to experience poverty than men, and occupational gender segregation contributes to this high poverty rate among women (Mclanahan, 2006).

We expect these financial and employment insecurities experienced by working-class women to lead them to develop a set of policy priorities that are distinct from both white-collar women and working-class men. First, we expect these insecurities to translate into a greater emphasis on government social welfare policy than both working-class men and white-collar women. The economic and employment vulnerabilities faced by working-class women may increase the salience of social welfare issues, leading them to prioritize these issues to compensate for their low earnings and job insecurity. Since both working-class men and women experience greater economic insecurity than their white-collar counterparts, they are likely to prioritize social welfare issues more highly. Working-class individuals face greater economic vulnerability when experiencing job loss and consequently tend to have higher levels of risk perceptions, compared to their high-skilled, white-collar counterparts (Chan and Goldthorpe, 2007; Rehm, 2009). This could lead to greater preference for expanding government-assisted social welfare programs, such as family assistance, disability services, and unemployment benefits, that can serve as crucial safety nets during economic hardships. Research explains class-based voting – the historical alignment of working-class voters with leftist parties – through these voters' strong preference for expanded government social welfare programs (Chan and Goldthorpe, 2007; Oesch, 2008).

However, given persistent gender division of labor within families and working-class women's greater reliance on government-funded care programs, we anticipate that working-class women will show even more concern about social welfare issues than working-class men. Previous research suggests that due to their greater domestic and care-related responsibilities, women tend to place particularly strong emphasis on government-funded social welfare programs than men (Anderson, 1999; Inglehart and Norris, 2003, Iversen & Rosenbluth, 2006). Since public assistance to childcare or elderly care opens more opportunities for women to seek outside employment by alleviating their traditional responsibilities (Iverson and Rosenbluth, 2006), women overall will exhibit higher levels of support for social welfare policies than men, regardless of socioeconomic status. Additionally, women's overrepresentation in pink-collar occupations, such as jobs in health and education sectors, contributes to wage inequalities experienced by these working-class women. Compared to traditionally male-dominated blue-collar jobs in manufacturing or technology sectors, these pink-collar sectors remain highly dependent on human labor with limited substitutability by capital. This feature can make working-class women employed in these sectors particularly vulnerable to wage suppression (Piketty, 2014). Following this line of logic, we expect working-class women to prioritize such issues more than their male counterparts with similar class backgrounds.

Women's tendency to prioritize social welfare issues more than men do should apply across class backgrounds. At the same time, when comparing women across social classes, working-class women are likely to demonstrate stronger preferences for social welfare programs than their white-collar counterparts, as they often rely more heavily on government-assisted care services, such as subsidized childcare. By guaranteeing a high income that allows for the purchase of private care services, white-collar job can meet women's demands for family-related social protection. However, working-class women are disproportionately employed in low-wage, low-security jobs and often cannot afford private options for care services. Additionally, many working-class women employed in service-sector jobs face nonstandard work schedules, making affordable, high-quality child and elderly care services even more difficult to access (Sandstrom and Chaudry, 2012). For these women, publicly financed care services would be a prominent, if not the most important, policy issue. This tendency will be relatively weaker among white-collar women with more secure jobs and higher earnings.

In addition, while many women, regardless of their class backgrounds consider family policy to be one of the most important issues in their lives, there may be stark differences in the types of family policies preferred by working-class and white-collar women. For example, even when workers have a legal right to parental leave, whether they actually have the opportunity to take it depends heavily on their income level and labor market status. Working-class women, who tend to earn low incomes and rely on precarious employment with fewer prospects for job mobility, may not be able to afford parental leave, unlike women in managerial or professional occupations (Javornik and Kurowska, 2017). These inequalities may lead to class differences in priorities for different types of family policies, with working-class women prioritizing immediate economic supports like government-assisted childcare subsidies or public daycare over parental leave policies that assume financial stability during unpaid periods. This preference reflects economic necessity, leading working-class women to place greater emphasis on direct government social welfare interventions compared to white-collar women, who typically have access to employer-provided benefits, paid leave options, and the financial resources to purchase private care alternatives.

We summarize this logic in the following hypotheses:

Hypothesis 3.1. Both working-class and white-collar women are more likely to prioritize social welfare than their male counterparts with similar class backgrounds.

Hypothesis 3.2. Both working-class men and women are more likely to prioritize social welfare than their white-collar counterparts.

Second, we expect working-class women to place greater emphasis on gender equality issues than white-collar women. We contend that women across social classes are more likely than men to emphasize government policies to expand gender equality, given the persistence of gender inequality in economic and social areas despite women's remarkable advancements in educational attainment and labor participation. At the same time, working-class women's greater vulnerability to gender-based economic inequalities might make this tendency more pronounced among them.

There exists a strong link between the gender pay gap and the structural wage penalty for female-dominated occupations. The literature on the gender pay gap shows considerable variation in the gender pay gap across sectors or occupations. In other words, the gender pay gap disproportionately affects women employed in certain sectors or occupations more than others. In particular, a large body of work has identified the structural wage penalty for female-dominated working-class occupations as a key factor contributing to the gender pay gap (Blau and Kahn, 1996; England et al., 1988; Huffman and Velasco, 1997; Tomaskovic-Devey et al., 2006). This trend reflects a long tradition of devaluing work typically performed by women (Acker, 1990; England, 2017). Taken together, these earlier findings suggest that countries with large gender wage gaps have a higher proportion of working-class women employed in pink-collar occupations, even though they face significant wage discrimination relative to other occupations.

Relatedly, research finds that gender differences in the wage gap are more pronounced in private sector jobs than in public sector jobs (Arulampalam et al., 2007; Gunderson, 1989). Given the tendency in the public sector to hire primarily educated, white-collar workers, this sectoral difference contributes to the greater gender wage discrimination faced by working-class women. In addition, the gender pay gap tends to be wider in low-paid jobs than in jobs in the middle of the wage distribution. This trend, referred to as the "sticky floor effect" (Arulampalam et al., 2007, 164), also contributes to the differential gender wage discrimination between working-class and white-collar women. We expect that working-class women's greater exposure to gender-based wage discrimination will increase their concern about gender-based inequality, motivating stronger support for policies aimed at promoting gender equality.

Hypothesis 3.3. Both working-class and white-collar women are more likely to prioritize gender equality policies than their male counterparts with similar class backgrounds.

Hypothesis 3.4. Working-class women are more likely to prioritize gender equality policies than white-collar women.

Next, we consider the conditions under which such class-based differences in women's policy priorities will be particularly prevalent. Specifically, we expect working-class women's tendency to prioritize social welfare or gender equality to become more pronounced as the gender wage gap widens. The existence of a large gender wage gap may increase the need of working-class women for government social welfare programs because working-class women experience higher levels of occupational and gender wage discrimination under such conditions. Research shows that the degree of occupational segregation by gender explains cross-country variation in the gender wage gap, even after accounting for differences in women's human capital (Herrera et al., 2019; Kim and Shirahase, 2014). This finding suggests that in countries with large gender wage inequalities, there will be more working-class women sorted into low-wage, low-security jobs. Based on these findings, we expect that the relative financial instability experienced by working-class women will be amplified in the presence of a high gender wage gap. These experiences could lead working-class women to prioritize policies to promote gender equality and women's rights more than white-collar women.

In a similar logic, working-class women's tendency to emphasize gender equality policies more than white-collar women will be more pronounced as gender wage gaps widen. Female-dominated pink-collar jobs, such as health aides or daycare teachers, typically receive significantly lower wages than gender-balanced or male-dominated occupations, a disparity attributed to the systematic devaluation of work done by women (England, 2010). In countries with large gender wage gaps, working-class women, who are overrepresented in these undervalued pink-collar jobs, experience more severe economic consequences from gender-based wage discrimination, making them more likely than their white-collar counterparts to prioritize gender equality policies.

Hypothesis 3.5. Working-class women are more likely to prioritize social welfare than working-class men or white-collar women when the gender wage gap is high.

Hypothesis 3.6. Working-class women are more likely to prioritize gender equality policies than working-class men or white-collar women when the gender wage gap is high.

3.3 Original Surveys in the United States and the UK

We first examine how patterns of women's policy priorities vary across their class backgrounds using original surveys in the United States and the UK. In October 2021 and February 2022, we fielded identical surveys in the United States and the UK, respectively.[3] Our surveys collected detailed occupational data by asking respondents to provide open-text descriptions of their current jobs and positions. Based on these responses, we categorized respondents into three groups: white-collar workers, working-class workers, and others (including retirees, stay-at-home caregivers, unemployed individuals, students, and people with disabilities). In classifying occupational categories, we follow Barnes et al.'s (2021) coding scheme, which provides a comprehensive list of jobs that make up working-class (either pink-collar or blue-collar) occupations. This coding scheme also serves as our reference for distinguishing between pink- and blue-collar occupations within the working class. In both surveys, the most common occupations among female respondents that were classified as working-class included retail clerk, secretary, nurse, childcare worker, and teacher – jobs traditionally categorized as "pink-collar" work. Among male respondents, working-class occupations were predominantly blue-collar jobs, such as machine operators and assembly workers.

To assess respondents' policy priorities, we included two questions in the surveys. The first asked respondents to select their most important policy areas from broad categories: economy, social welfare, child/family, gender equality, racial equality, health, and education. While child and family policy is often considered a subgroup of the broad category of social welfare, we included it as a separate category to gauge respondents' emphasis on this specific aspect of social policy. The second question delved deeper, presenting specific policy agendas within six domains: economy, gender equality, health, social welfare, education, and public safety.[4] The two questions also differed in the number of

---

[3] Participants from the United States were recruited via Lucid's online research platform, while UK participants were recruited through Prolific.
[4] In the economy area, the issues include consumer prices, retirement and investment, national budget, taxation, and unemployment. Under gender equality, there are gender wage gaps, LGBTQ + rights, reproductive rights, and violence against women. Health care includes access to medical care and health insurance, prescription drug pricing, and management of the COVID-19 pandemic. Social welfare includes assistance for low-income families, support for people with disabilities, childcare assistance, elderly assistance programs, and parental leave. For education, categories include public school funding, quality of public education, student loan debt, and

options respondents could select: the first question asked respondents to select a single policy area, while the second question allowed them to choose three policy issues, enabling us to capture their diverse policy priorities. Offering options for detailed policy proposals is particularly useful for understanding one's priorities regarding social welfare programs, as priorities over specific social welfare programs might vary substantially across individuals. Research demonstrates that public attitudes toward social welfare policies vary significantly based on how these policies are framed and which aspects of social welfare are emphasized in the policy discourse. Notably, studies in the United States reveal the complexity in how Americans view social welfare. While many Americans oppose expanding government welfare programs in general, they tend to support the idea of helping the poor or programs that are designed to assist the poor (Feldman and Zaller, 1992, Henry et al., 2004). There's also a clear divide in support based on the type of beneficiaries: Americans typically favor universal programs that benefit the elderly or disabled (like Social Security and Medicare) but show less support for means-tested programs such as the Supplemental Nutrition Assistance Program (SNAP, formerly food stamps) or Temporary Assistance for Needy Families (TANF) (Weaver et al., 1995), often driven by racial attitudes (Gilens, 2009). Since our primary focus is examining how social welfare policy preferences and priorities vary by socio-economic background, we analyze a broad range of social programs. These include family-oriented policies (such as childcare and parental leave assistance), means-tested programs (such as support for low-income families), and programs supporting the elderly or disabled.

Tables 5 and 6 display the policy priorities of respondents in our US and UK surveys, respectively, broken down by gender and class background. The analysis reported in these tables excludes non-employed individuals (retirees, homemakers, students, those with disabilities, and unemployed persons) in each sample. There are several discernable gendered patterns. First, consistent with previous research, men prioritize economic issues more than women but show less interest in social welfare (Andersen, 1999; Funk and Gathmann, 2015). Second, women in general place greater emphasis on child/family policies compared to men with similar backgrounds. One exception is working-class men in the United States, who emphasize child/family policy at higher rates than working-class women in the same sample. Turning to class-based differences, we do not find much support for our expectations that working-class women will be more likely to prioritize social welfare, particularly family

---

education of underserved students. Finally, under public safety, there are crime prevention and gun control policy (US only).

Table 5 Share of prioritize policy by gender and class (US survey)

	Men ($N = 398$)		Women ($N = 448$)	
	White-Collar (%)	Working-Class (%)	White-Collar (%)	Working-Class (%)
Economy	51.7	53.4	34.9	35.5
Social Welfare	6.15	5.48	11.1	9.68
Child/Family	7.38	13.7	12	8.06
Gender Equality	2.77	4.11	3.4	7.26
Racial Equality	6.77	6.85	8.3	14.5
Health	21.2	13.7	28.1	20.2
Education	4	2.74	2.16	4.84
Chi-squared (p-value)	5.172 (0.522)		12.278[+] (0.056)	
Observation	325	73	324	124

Note: + $p < 0.10$

Table 6 Share of prioritize policy by gender and class (UK survey)

	Men ($N = 290$)		Women ($N = 673$)	
	White-Collar (%)	Working-Class (%)	White-Collar (%)	Working-Class (%)
Economy	50.4	34.8	31.8	22.8
Social Welfare	14.3	21.2	20.3	18.8
Child/Family	3.57	6.06	14	18.3
Gender Equality	0.89	1.52	1.78	3.12
Racial Equality	1.79	3.03	2	3.12
Health	25.9	27.3	26.9	25.9
Education	3.12	6.06	3.12	8.04
Chi-Squared (p-value)	6.718 (0.348)		15.877* (0.014)	
Observations	224	66	440	224

Note: * $p < 0.05$

policy, than white-collar women in our US survey. In this sample, a greater share of white-collar women said they prioritize social welfare or child/family policy than working-class women. In the UK sample, on the other hand, we find that a greater share of working-class women prioritizes child/family issue than white-collar women. The share of respondents prioritizing social welfare over other issues is slightly larger among white-collar women than working-class women. Pearson's chi-squared test results suggest that the relationship between class background and policy priority is statistically significant at 0.1 level for women respondents but not for men in the US study. The same pattern appears in the UK study, where the relationship between class background and policy priority is statistically significant at 0.05 level for women but not for men.

Two additional differences between the two groups merit attention. First, working-class women placed higher priority on education across both surveys. Second, particularly in our US survey, they showed stronger emphasis on gender equality and racial equality compared to white-collar women. The strong emphasis on racial equality likely reflects the racial diversity among working-class women in our sample. In our US sample, 36% of working-class women identified as women of color (Black, Latina, Native American, or Asian). This racial composition aligns with broader labor market patterns in the United States, where Black and Latina women are disproportionately represented in working-class (particularly pink-collar) occupations, highlighting the importance of examining racial implications of class-based divisions in policy preferences.[5] Overall, these findings partially support our theoretical framework regarding class-based variations in women's policy priorities.

Next, we analyze the second policy priority question that offered more specific issue areas for options. We focus first on social welfare issues, examining how class and gender intersect in shaping preferences within this domain. The second policy priority question asked respondents to list three policy issues they prioritize, and Tables 7 and 8 display the percentage of respondents who included each policy issue among their three highest policy priorities. While our US survey reveals clear gender differences in social welfare policy preferences, we found less evidence of the theorized class distinctions among women. We find that women overall prioritize family and elderly assistance more than men, though both genders place similar emphasis on government childcare support in our US sample. White-collar and working-class women do not show meaningful differences in their emphasis of specific welfare policy programs. White-collar women slightly favor assistance for low-income families and disabled/elderly support, while working-class women emphasize childcare assistance. However, these differences are not statistically significant. Our UK survey reveals more consistent class-based patterns in women's policy priorities than the US data. Table 8 shows working-class women prioritize assistance for low-income families,

---

[5] For racial makeups of working-class individuals, see, for example, www.epi.org/publication/the-changing-demographics-of-americas-working-class/.

Table 7 Share of respondents who listed each policy issue as one of their priorities (by class and gender; US survey)

	Men		Women	
	White-Collar (%)	Working-Class (%)	White-Collar (%)	Working-Class (%)
Assistance to Low-Income Families	8.6	6.9	13	10.5
p-value:	(0.600)		(0.458)	
Assistance to the Disabled	8.62	4.11	8.02	6.45
p-value:	(0.111)		(0.558)	
Childcare Assistance	4.3	5.48	4.32	5.65
p-value:	(0.688)		(0.577)	
Elderly Assistance	4.31	6.85	8.95	7.26
p-value:	(0.427)		(0.550)	
Parental Leave	1.2	0	0.3	3.23
p-value:	(0.045)*		(0.075)+	
Gender Equal Pay	7.38	1.37	7.41	6.45
p-value:	(0.003)**		(0.719)	
Abortion Rights	12.3	11	20.1	28.2
p-value:	(0.743)		(0.079)+	
N	325	73	324	124

Note: $+\, p < 0.1$; $*\, p < 0.05$; $**\, p < 0.01$

Table 8 Share of respondents who listed each policy issue as one of their priorities (by class and gender; UK Survey)

	Men		Women	
	White-Collar (%)	Working-Class (%)	White-Collar (%)	Working-Class (%)
Assistance to Low-Income Families	17.4	22.7	20.9	22.8
p-value:	(0.360)		(0.591)	
Assistance to the Disabled	4.91	9.09	6.90	8.93
p-value:	(0.280)		(0.370)	
Childcare Assistance	4.02	0	6.68	9.82
p-value:	(0.003)**		(0.176)	

Table 8 (cont.)

	Men		Women	
	White-Collar (%)	Working-Class (%)	White-Collar (%)	Working-Class (%)
Elderly Assistance	4.02	4.55	6.68	7.14
p-value:	(0.856)		(0.825)	
Parental Leave	0	0	3.34	2.23
p-value:			(0.396)	
Gender Equal Pay	4.91	9.09	12	8.04
p-value:	(0.280)		(0.094)+	
Abortion Rights	0.89	1.52	4.01	6.7
p-value:	(0.705)		(0.161)	
N	224	66	440	224

Note: $+ p < 0.1$; $* p < 0.05$; $** p < 0.01$

disabled individuals, elderly care, and childcare at higher rates than white-collar women, though these differences do not reach statistical significance. In both surveys, more women than men emphasized abortion policies, a pattern consistent with recent research on this topic (Cassese et al., 2025).

In addition, noticeable class-based differences appear in gender equality policy agendas. In both US and UK samples, working-class women prioritized abortion rights more than white-collar women. Over 28% of working-class women in the US survey included abortion rights among their policy priorities, compared to 20% of white-collar women. This difference is statistically significant at $p < 0.1$ ($p = 0.079$). White-collar women, by contrast, prioritize policies to promote gender equal pay at a higher rate than working-class women in both surveys.

The analyses of our original surveys in the United States and the UK reveal several important patterns about class and gender dynamics in policy priorities. We theorized that working-class women will prioritize child and family policies more than white-collar women. This pattern holds in our UK survey, but not in US data. This difference may emerge from how child and family policies operate differently in these countries. Over recent years, the UK government has substantially expanded its role in childcare, aiming for universal access to affordable childcare (Gray and Francis, 2007; Penn, 2007). For instance, all working parents in the UK are entitled to 30 hours of free childcare through government assistance.[6] US child-care assistance is more fragmented and limited in scope

---

[6] Source: https://ifstudies.org/blog/britain-is-heading-towards-universal-child-care

compared to the UK, lagging behind almost all other OECD countries in its child care provisions (Durfee and Meyers, 2006). This difference may lead to the relatively lower public attention to government's role in childcare in the United States, accounting for the lack of class-based differences in prioritizing this issue.

Our analysis also demonstrates significant differences between working-class and white-collar women in their attitudes toward gender equality policies. Overall, working-class women tend to prioritize gender equality issue more than white-collar women do, with a particular emphasis on abortion rights. While this analysis offers suggestive evidence for class-based divisions in women's policy priorities, we complement this largely descriptive analysis based on small-N samples with a comprehensive cross-national survey analysis in the next section.

3.4 Cross-national Study

Data and Measures

We empirically test our arguments about class-based divisions using the Comparative Study of Electoral System (CSES) datasets, which pool post-election surveys from over 30 countries since 1996. To measure policy priorities, we use Module 3 (2006–2011) of the CSES, which has a unique set of questions that measure respondents' policy priorities and preferred policy positions across a wide range of issues. In particular, we use respondents' answers to the question asking about the most important issue to the respondent personally in the most recent election. The response options to this question varied considerably across countries to reflect country-specific contexts. To make the responses comparable across countries, we recoded them based on a simplified classification of policy areas. The categories are: abortion, education, environment, family policy, foreign policy, gender, health care, immigration, labor, national economy, pensions, personal finance, politics, public resources, security, social justice, social welfare, taxes, and values. The dataset covers 35 unique countries with diverse political, social, and economic contexts. This broad coverage allows us to examine how class and gender differences in policy priorities emerge in different socioeconomic contexts. Specifically, we can test how gender wage inequality affects the political priorities of working-class women, as suggested by our hypotheses.

Our explanatory variables are respondents' gender and class background. We identify respondents' class backgrounds based on their occupations, following a standard approach in the literature. The CSES does not provide information on individual respondents' specific occupations, so we cannot accurately categorize respondents' occupations into blue-collar, white-collar, and pink-collar occupations, as we did in our previous analysis. Instead, it provides occupational information based on skill level and skill specialization using a two-digit International Standard Classification of Occupations (ISCO-08) code, which allows us to group respondents' occupations into high-skilled and low-skilled jobs. Low-skilled jobs include elementary occupations such as many low-paid and entry-level service sector jobs, routine and manual jobs such as cleaners, helpers, food preparation assistants, and low-skilled workers in mining, construction, agriculture, forestry, and fishing. These jobs largely overlap with blue-collar and white-collar jobs. High-skilled jobs are mostly white-collar jobs, including managerial, senior administrative, and professional jobs.

Figure 6 shows the distribution of respondents' policy priorities by class background. We begin by presenting the responses of female respondents. Women in high-skilled occupations place the highest priority on the national economy, followed by personal finance, politics, health care, and education. Figure 7 shows that class women have a similar ranking of policy priorities: their policy priorities are in the order of national economy, politics, personal finance, health care and education. As shown in Figure 8, when only social welfare is considered, a larger proportion of working-class women prioritize this issue compared to white-collar women. Similarly, more working-class men place the highest priority on social welfare than their white-collar counterparts, though this difference is less pronounced than among women. Figure 8 also demonstrates that more women prioritize social welfare than men regardless of their class background.

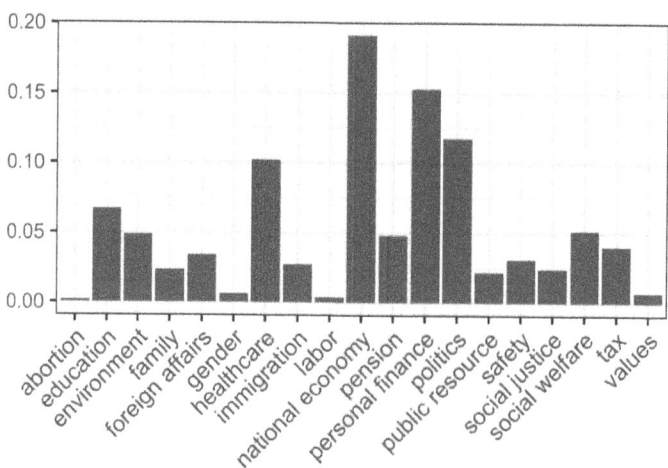

Figure 6 Policy priority of women with high-skill occupations

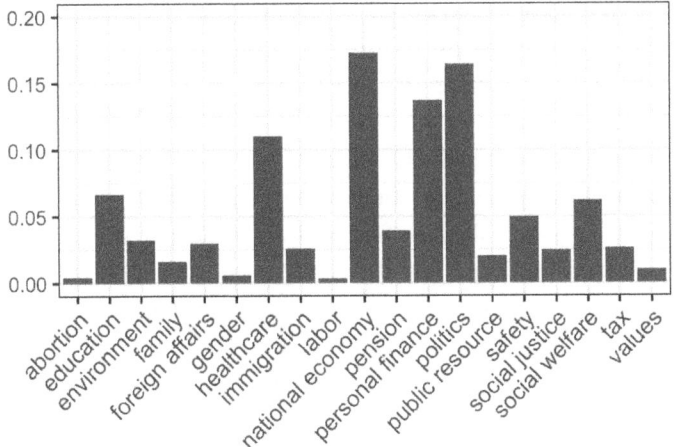

Figure 7 Policy priority of women with low-skill occupations

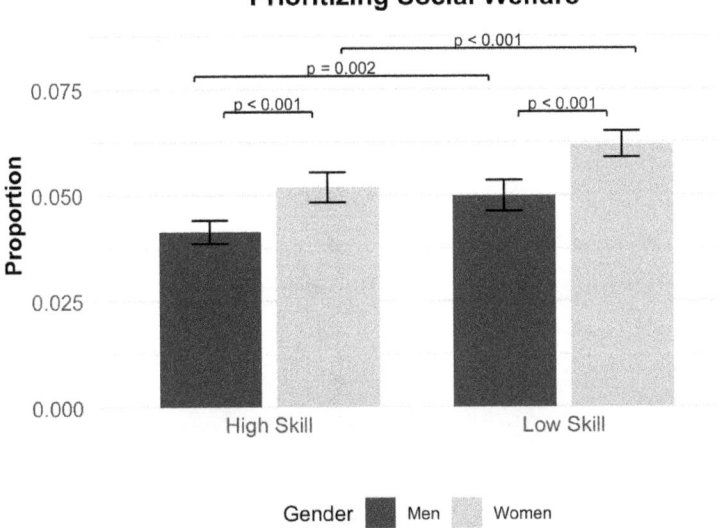

Figure 8 Proportion of CSES respondents prioritizing social welfare (by gender and skill level)

3.5 Findings

While the findings from the previous section suggests some evidence of class-based differences in policy priorities among women, we now turn to a more systematic comparison of the policy priorities of white-collar and blue-collar women. To test our hypotheses, we fit multilevel logistic models with Social Welfare Priority as the outcome variable and survey from all countries in the dataset. The outcome variable of interest, Social Welfare Priority, is operationalized as a binary variable that takes on a value of 1 if the respondent listed social welfare issues as a political priority.

Our explanatory variables are an individual's gender and class background. We create a binary variable, *Low Skill*, coded 1 if the individual has low-skill, working-class occupations and 0 if the individual has high-skill occupations. We control for individual-level characteristics, including educational attainment, age, household income, political ideology, unemployment status, and marital status. In addition, we include country-level variables, including the level of democracy and GDP growth rates, as control variables in our models. These country-level variables are provided by the CSES. These country-level variables are lagged by one year to capture their effect over time. We also include country fixed effects in our models to account for other country-specific characteristics, while allowing the intercepts to vary across countries by fitting a multilevel random intercept model.

In Figure 9, we report the odds ratios from the logistic regression with 95% confidence intervals. The results first show that female respondents are more likely to prioritize social welfare than male respondents, consistent with the expectations of previous studies (Andersen, 1999; Inglehart and Norris, 2003).

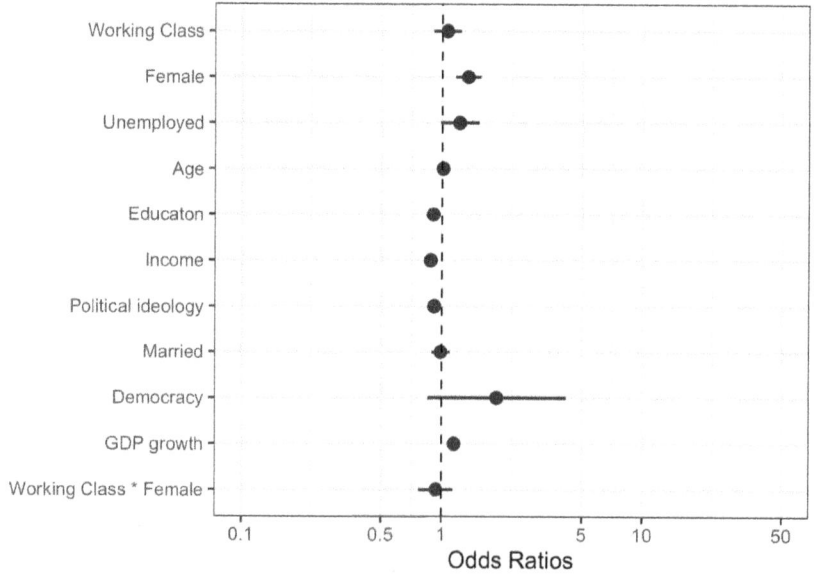

Figure 9 The likelihood of prioritizing social welfare (all countries)

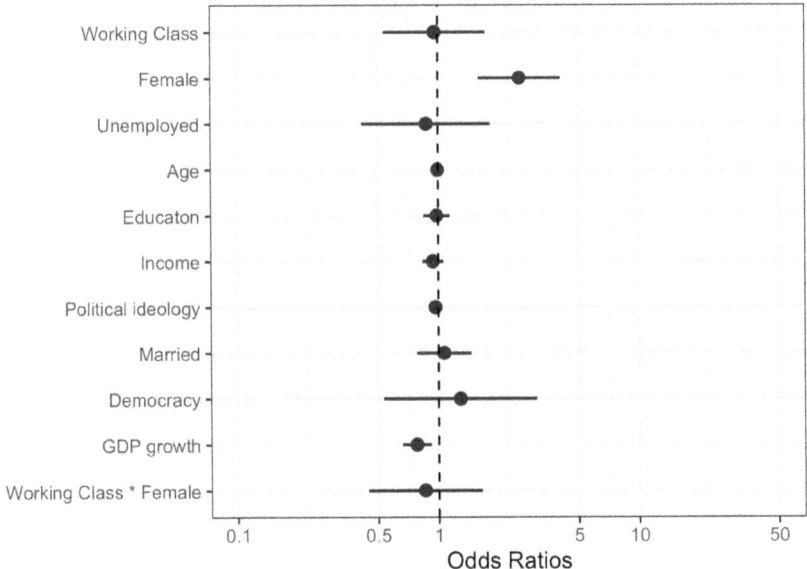

Figure 10 The likelihood of prioritizing gender equality (all countries)

However, in this pooled model we find no statistically significant effect of the interaction term between female and low skill. This suggests that contrary to our theoretical expectation in Hypothesis 3.2, low-skilled women are not more likely to prioritize social welfare than other class-gender groups when we pool all countries. Similarly, Figure 10 shows that working-class women are not more likely than white-collar women to prioritize gender equality policies, failing to confirm our Hypothesis 3.4.

Figure 11 shows the distribution of the gender pay gap for each country in our sample. The measure comes from the OECD and indicates the difference between the median full-time earnings of men and women, relative to the median full-time earnings of men. To account for the gradual effect of the gender pay gap, we use a one-year lagged measure. The mean of the gender pay gap in our sample is 17.021, which means that, on average, a woman earning the median full-time wage earns 83 cents for every dollar earned by a man earning the median full-time wage. There is considerable variation in the gender pay gap across the countries in our sample. South Korea and Japan have the highest gender pay gaps (38.2 and 33, respectively), while countries such as Chile, New Zealand, Greece, and Norway have gender pay gaps below 10.

Using this information on the cross-country gender pay gap, we next turn to test our next set of hypotheses, where we expect to find different levels of class-based differences in policy priorities depending on the gender pay gap. First, we

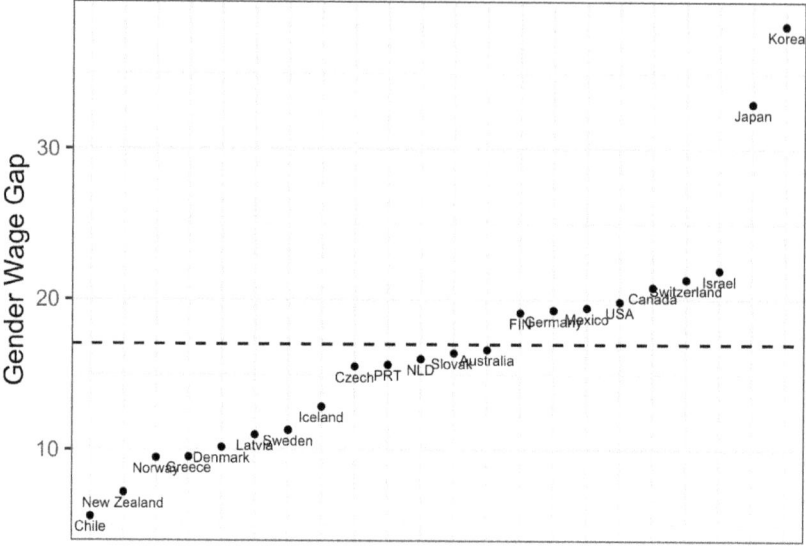

Figure 11 Gender wage gap by country

Note: The dashed line represents the mean of the gender wage gap in our sample (=17.021).

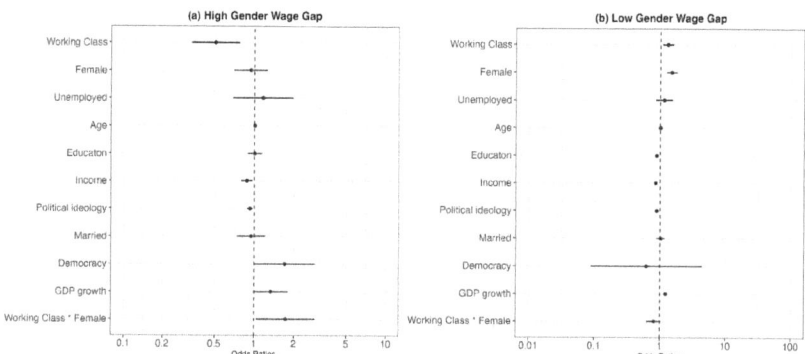

Figure 12 The likelihood of prioritizing social welfare

use a subset of countries where the gender pay gap is larger than the mean. These countries include Canada, Switzerland, Germany, Finland, Israel, Japan, South Korea, Mexico, and the United States. The results are shown in the left panel of Figure 12. Interestingly, individuals in low-skilled occupations, both men and women combined, are less likely to prioritize social welfare than others in countries with large gender wage gaps, as suggested by the statistically

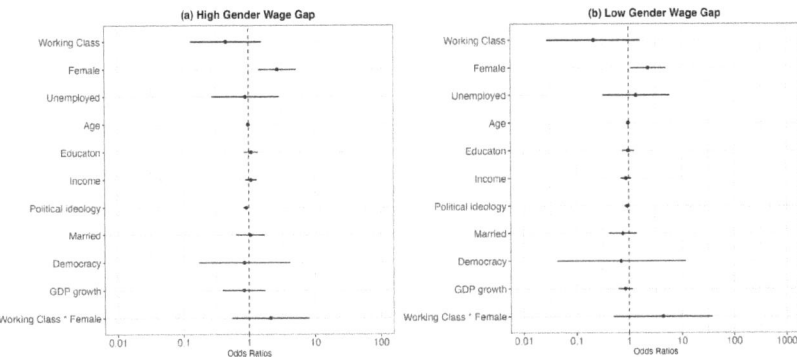

Figure 13 The likelihood of prioritizing gender equality

significant and negative odds ratio for *Low Skill*. Also, the likelihood of prioritizing social welfare does not differ between male and female respondents in these countries. At the same time, we see that the interaction term between *Low Skill* and *Female* is statistically significant and positive. This indicates that women are more likely to prioritize social welfare than men only when we compare low-skilled, working-class individuals. In other words, in the presence of high gender wage inequalities, low-skilled women are more likely to prioritize social welfare than men with comparable skill levels, while this gender gap does not appear for high-skilled individuals. When only those countries with a relatively low gender pay gap are considered, the combined effect of *Female* and *Low Skill* disappears, as shown in the right panel of Figure 12. This finding offers support to Hypothesis 3.5.

Figure 13 shows how respondent characteristics influence the likelihood of prioritizing gender equality policies, comparing high versus low gender wage gap countries. We found no significant differences in the likelihood of prioritizing gender equality policies between countries with high versus low gender wage gaps, failing to confirm Hypothesis 3.6.

3.6 Summary and Implications

In this section, we laid out a theoretical framework that links differential socioeconomic conditions experienced by different class and gender groups to their policy priorities. We first expected that the financial vulnerability faced by working-class women will lead them to prioritize social welfare issues, particularly family policy, over other concerns, and that this tendency will be greater in societies with larger gender pay gaps, where such financial difficulties are magnified. We further hypothesized that the greater gender-based inequalities experienced by working-class women will translate into prioritization of gender equality issues.

Through original surveys conducted in the United States and the UK, we examined how women's policy priorities vary by their class backgrounds, measured by open-ended responses about their occupations. Our UK survey shows working-class women tend to prioritize family policy more than white-collar women. This tendency is weaker among our US respondents. In both surveys, working-class women prioritize gender equality at a higher rate than their white-collar counterparts. Our results using CSES data provide partial support for our hypotheses. While working-class women are no more likely to prioritize social welfare than upper-class women, they are significantly more likely to do so than working-class men in the presence of large gender wage gaps. This gender difference in countries with large gender wage gaps does not appear among non-working-class individuals. These findings suggest that economic inequalities between men and women have a greater impact on working-class women and shape the policy areas they prioritize in ways that do not apply to white-collar women. Additionally, this finding suggests an important implication for understanding policy priorities of working-class men. The wider gender gap in social welfare prioritization among working-class individuals in countries with large gender wage inequalities may be driven by working-class men, who become less likely to prioritize social welfare when gender wage gaps are high. While working-class men generally prioritize social welfare issues more than their white-collar counterparts, this tendency appears to diminish in systems with severe gender-based inequalities. This suggests that economic inequality along gender lines may reshape traditional class-based policy preferences.

Taken together, our findings in this section suggest mixed perspectives on the class-based differences in policy priorities among women. While we identify some divergences between working-class and white-collar women's policy priorities, these class distinctions are less pronounced than gender-based differences in other policy areas. Nevertheless, our findings provide several important insights into the intersectional approach to understanding citizens' policy priorities. First, our descriptive analysis of CSES data indicates that working-class women prioritize social welfare issues at higher rates than any other gender-class subgroup. This pattern aligns with our theoretical expectation that the unique working and living conditions experienced by working-class women lead them to place greater emphasis on government social welfare programs.

Second, our findings underscore that women's class backgrounds shape their policy priorities in nuanced ways that vary across national contexts. In particular, our findings suggest that systematic gender inequalities deepen these class-based differences, as working-class women are disproportionately affected by gender-based economic inequalities. Future research can further explore how different political and policy environments may reduce or exacerbate the financial vulnerability of working-class women, potentially shaping class-based differences in policy priorities and preferences.

Finally, our findings indicate that class background correlates with other demographic factors that influence financial circumstances and policy priorities. As shown by our US sample, working-class occupations tend to overrepresent racial and ethnic minorities, particularly among women. This racial composition among working-class women explains their stronger focus on racial equality issues than white-collar women's focus. It is crucial for future research to explore how the class-based differences in policy attitudes we have identified operate differently across racial groups.

4 How Class and Gender Interact to Shape Political Attitudes

4.1 The Impact of Economic Insecurity on Political Efficacy and Engagement

Section 3 examines how class and gender identities jointly shape policy preferences, highlighting the dynamic interplay between socioeconomic status and gender in influencing political attitudes and behaviors. This section extends the discussion by demonstrating that the intersection of class and gender significantly affects not only policy preferences but also political behavior, including attitudes toward politics, political engagement, and voting choices.

A wealth of prior research has documented the detrimental effects of lower economic status and economic insecurity on political attitudes. Economic precarity, characterized by unstable income, job insecurity, and limited access to financial resources, fosters perceived vulnerability that undermines trust in political systems. For instance, individuals in precarious economic conditions are more likely to perceive governments as unresponsive or indifferent to their needs (Chi et al., 2013). This erosion of political trust often translates into diminished confidence in governmental accountability and competence, further lowering external political efficacy – the belief that one's actions can influence political outcomes (Barnes and Saxton, 2019; Norris, 2015).

These negative perceptions of government efficacy and fairness have far-reaching consequences. For economically disadvantaged individuals, feelings of disenfranchisement often manifest as political disengagement, resulting in higher rates of voter abstention. Alternatively, when they do participate, they are likely to vote against traditional political establishments, leading to protest voting and increased support for radical and populist parties that claim to represent marginalized voices (Emmenegger et al., 2015; Kweon, 2018; Marx and Picot, 2013). These trends show that economic insecurity can drive individuals' sense of political alienation and their political radicalization. Importantly, appealing to this sense of political alienation, radical parties tend to nominate more working-class candidates than traditional center-left and center-right parties (Matthews and Kerevel, 2022).

In addition to influencing attitudes, economic precarity affects individuals' capacity to engage in political activities. Stable jobs and workplaces often serve as crucial sites for political socialization, providing individuals with exposure to political discussions, opportunities to advocate for shared interests, and access to resources that foster political efficacy. Regular employment not only helps individuals develop political interests but also connects them to networks that encourage participation in civic and political life. In contrast, those in insecure or irregular jobs, as well as individuals without paid occupations, often lack these critical opportunities and resources. This absence of social capital and institutional support leaves economically marginalized individuals at a disadvantage in developing political interests or a sense of efficacy (Iversen and Rosenbluth 2006; 2008).

In this section, we further argue that the impact of economic precarity is often compounded by gender. Women in lower economic strata frequently face unique challenges due to societal norms and structural barriers that further limit their access to political and economic opportunities. Precarious employment or unpaid caregiving roles disproportionately affect women, reducing their exposure to politically enriching environments and curtailing their ability to participate in political activities. These compounded effects underscore the intersection of class and gender as a critical lens for understanding variations in political behavior and attitudes. By exploring these dynamics, Section 4 sheds light on the ways in which class and gender intersect to shape broader patterns of political efficacy and participation.

4.2 Theory and Hypotheses

While the underprivileged generally exhibit more negative attitudes toward politics, including lower political efficacy and diminished trust in government, we argue that the negative effects of working-class backgrounds are more pronounced among female voters than their male counterparts. Working-class women face dual challenges arising from their disadvantaged gender and class status, which shape their political experiences in unique and often compounding ways. Economic challenges such as wage gaps and job insecurity disproportionately impact women, amplifying their political alienation. Across many countries, women are more likely than men to experience precarious employment conditions, including part-time jobs and temporary contracts. These economic vulnerabilities often translate into reduced access to the resources and networks necessary for political engagement, deepening feelings of disconnection from the political system. As a result, the interplay of gender and class introduces multiple layers of barriers that affect not only attitudes toward politics but also toward democracy.

Different class effects on political attitudes by gender can also be explained by disparities in perceived political representation and accountability. In most democracies, political representation is overwhelmingly skewed toward white-collar individuals and the economically privileged. Studies have consistently demonstrated that this underrepresentation of the working-class has substantive policy consequences, as politicians from affluent backgrounds are less likely to support policies that benefit economically disadvantaged populations (Carnes, 2012; Barnes et al., 2021; O'Grady, 2019). The absence of working-class voices in politics weakens the belief among economically marginalized individuals that they can influence politics or that governments will be responsive to their needs (Atkeson & Carrillo, 2007; Phillips, 1995). It also erodes trust in government (Mansbridge, 1999). For working-class women, these representation issues are even more pronounced. While the visibility of women in politics has increased over recent decades, this progress has largely been confined to women from white-collar backgrounds. The challenges and priorities of white-collar women often diverge significantly from those of their working-class counterparts. As a result, the rise in women's descriptive representation has had a limited, if not negative, effect on the political efficacy of working-class women (Kweon, 2024).

Although the underrepresentation of the working class is a pervasive issue affecting both male and female representatives, we argue that it has a greater impact on female voters. This is because women voters tend to place higher expectations on female representatives to prioritize and advocate for policies that address women's unique challenges (Bauer, 2017; Dolan, 2003; Gay, 2002; Herrnson et al., 2003; Jones, 2014). The presence of female politicians often signals to women voters that these representatives will be more accountable to them and will prioritize policies that address women's concerns. However, when female politicians – many of whom come from white-collar backgrounds – fail to represent the interests of working-class women, it creates a profound sense of disillusionment. Such high expectation creates a bigger room for disappointment when these female politicians appear to be far out of touch from the world many working-class women live in (Kweon, 2024; Kim and Kweon, 2024). To the extent that women's policy priorities diverge depending on their class backgrounds as demonstrated in Section 3, female representatives, most of whom come from white-collar backgrounds, will fail to advance policy agendas prioritized by pink-collar women. In other words, the overrepresentation of white-collar individuals among female representatives may create a class-based representation gap. This discrepancy, in turn, could undermine working-class women's sense of political efficacy.

By contrast, male politicians are not typically subject to such gendered expectations of representation and accountability. The political arena has long been perceived as a masculine domain, with male politicians embodying the normative model of political leadership (Eagly and Karau, 2002; Koenig et al., 2011). Consequently, male politicians are evaluated primarily on factors other than their gender, such as their policies, party affiliation, or leadership style. This absence of gendered expectations means that male voters are less likely to condition their political attitudes on the perceived representational qualities of male politicians. As a result, the effect of working-class underrepresentation among male voters is not mediated by the gender of political representatives (Jones, 2014; Kweon, 2024).

Based on the discussions earlier, we argue that working-class backgrounds will have a more pronounced negative impact on women's political attitudes and voting choices compared to men's. Women from working-class backgrounds often face dual challenges of socioeconomic and gender-based disadvantages, which can amplify their skepticism toward politics and democracy. These disadvantages are not only material such as limited economic resources, but also symbolic, stemming from the absence of representation and accountability that marginalize working-class women in politics. As a result, these women are likely to feel alienated from mainstream politics, perceiving them as elitist, male-dominated, and unresponsive to their needs. This alienation often manifests in low political efficacy, with many working-class women feeling that their voices do not matter in political decision-making processes. Consequently, their satisfaction with democracy tends to be lower, as they may view democratic systems as perpetuating inequality rather than addressing their concerns.

In terms of voting behavior, this disenchantment can lead working-class women to disengage from electoral participation altogether, resulting in higher rates of voter withdrawal. For those who do choose to vote, these women are more likely to support nontraditional or antiestablishment parties. In particular, radical right-wing parties may appeal to these women by positioning themselves as challengers to the status quo and promising to disrupt the dominance of established parties that working-class women perceive as neglecting their interests. Such parties often employ rhetoric that resonates with the frustrations of marginalized groups, even if their policies do not necessarily align with the long-term interests of these voters (Mudde, 2007; Mudde and Rovira Kaltwasser, 2018).

In contrast to women, numerous studies have shown that radical right-wing parties receive greater support from men and are often characterized by antifeminist rhetoric, frequently labeled as "men's parties" or *Männerparteien* (Mudde, 2007). Given their dominant social status, men may be especially sensitive to perceived disruptions to the existing social order posed by outgroups such as women and immigrants, regardless of their class position (Krook, 2016; Mansbridge and Shames, 2008). Parallel research also demonstrates that individuals experiencing economic vulnerability are more likely to support populist movements (Gest et al., 2018; Kweon, 2018; Marx, 2014). However, relatively few studies investigate how gender and class intersect in shaping support for radical right-wing politics. In particular, the political behavior of working-class women remains largely absent from this literature. Addressing this gap, we argue that while economic insecurity generally increases support for radical right-wing parties, the effect of class is more pronounced among women than among men – such that working-class women are more likely to support these parties compared to white-collar women, whereas men's support is less differentiated by class.

Building on the discussions earlier, we propose four hypotheses to examine how working-class backgrounds influence political efficacy and related attitudes differently based on voters' gender. The first hypothesis suggests that the negative impact of working-class backgrounds on political efficacy will be greater for women than for men, reflecting the challenges faced by working-class women in political engagement. The second hypothesis posits that economic backgrounds have gendered effects on democratic satisfaction. Economic challenges and insecurity that disproportionately affect women could not only affect the beliefs about their political influence and democratic accountability, but also their satisfaction with democracy. The remaining two hypotheses focus on voting behavior. The third hypothesis extends the argument about political efficacy, predicting that the negative effects of working-class backgrounds will lead to lower voting participation among women compared to men. Lastly, the fourth hypothesis predicts that working-class backgrounds are more likely to drive women, more so than men, toward supporting radical right-wing parties as a form of protest against a status quo that fails to address their concerns. These hypotheses aim to shed light on the intersection of class, gender, and political engagement.

Hypothesis 1: *The negative effect of working-class backgrounds on political efficacy will be bigger for women than men.*

Hypothesis 2: *The negative effect of working-class backgrounds on democratic satisfaction will be bigger for women than men.*

Hypothesis 3: *The negative effect of working-class backgrounds on vote abstention will be bigger for women than men.*

Hypothesis 4: *The positive effect of working-class backgrounds on voting support for radical right-wing parties will be bigger for women than men.*

4.3 Data and Measures

We test our hypotheses using both cross-national and panel data. For cross-national data, we will draw on Modules 1–5 of the Comparative Study of Electoral System datasets. For political efficacy as dependent variables, we focus on two measures: internal efficacy and external efficacy. For internal efficacy, we use an item that measures respondents' belief that voting makes difference. For external efficacy, we use an item that measures respondents' belief that who is in power matters. These are two widely used items for political efficacy (see Karp and Banducci, 2008). In order to further examine the implications for democracy, we additionally use an item that measures respondents' satisfaction of democracy in their countries. The two measures of political efficacy use a 5-point scale, while the measure for democratic satisfaction uses a 4-point scale. For comparability, we recode the three variables to binary variables.

For voting attitudes, we examine two key variables: voting abstention and support for radical right-wing parties, both measured as binary outcomes. The abstention variable is coded as 1 if an individual did not vote in the most recent general election and 0 otherwise. Support for radical right-wing parties is coded as 1 if an individual voted for a party classified as radical right-wing, and 0 otherwise. The classification of radical right-wing parties is based on the party ideological families categorized by CSES. Parties that are categorized as ethnocentric or nationalist are coded as radical right-wing parties.

For key independent and conditioning variables, we use binary measures for respondents' gender (female = 1, male = 0) and occupational skill (low-skill = 1, high-skill = 0) for independent variables. Figure 14 illustrates the percentage of low-skilled workers by gender. As previously discussed, women are significantly more likely than men to hold low-skilled jobs. While less than 40% of men are employed in low-skilled occupations, this figure exceeds 50% for women. This indicates that, on average, the majority of women are engaged in low-skilled work, leaving them more vulnerable to economic precarity and lower economic status. We additionally control several

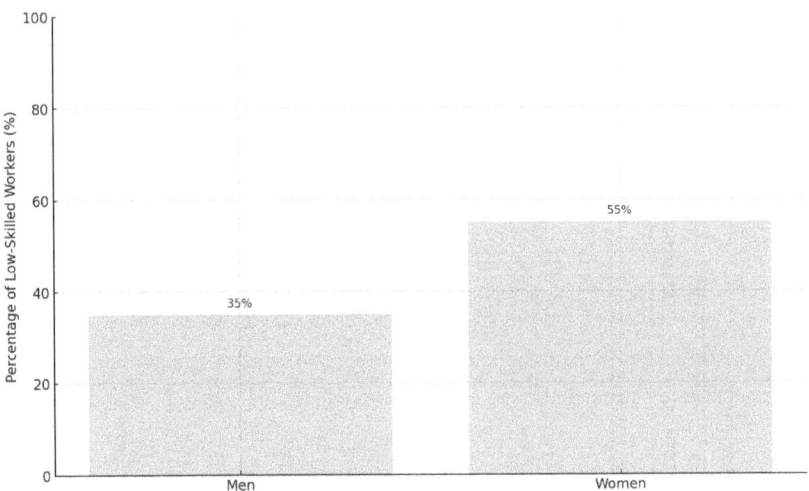

Figure 14 Share of low-skilled workers by gender

individual- and macro-level variables including educational levels, household income, age, political ideology, unemployment status, levels of democracy, and GDP growth rates. All macro-level variables are lagged by one year.

For empirical modeling, we employ a multilevel logistic regression approach with random intercepts for countries to account for the hierarchical structure of our data, which includes both individual- and country-level variables. This method is particularly well suited for our analysis as it allows us to simultaneously model the effects of variables at different levels while accounting for the clustering of individuals within countries. The random intercepts capture unobserved heterogeneity across countries, ensuring that country-specific factors, such as cultural, political, or institutional contexts, do not bias our estimates.

4.4 Findings for Political Efficacy and Democratic Satisfaction

Table 9 shows the results of our empirical analysis. Columns (1) and (2) display the effects on respondents' belief that vote makes difference (internal efficacy), columns (3) and (4) the effects on the belief that who is in power matters (external efficacy), and the last two columns (5) and (6) the effects on democratic satisfaction. As presented in columns (1), (3), and (5), we first examined the independent effects of gender and class. For all three dependent variables, our results show that being a woman or having a low-skilled occupation have negative impacts on political efficacy and satisfaction with democracy, and their impacts are statistically significant. Both women and working-class individuals are less likely to believe that vote makes difference and that who is in power

Table 9 Effects on political efficacy and democratic satisfaction

	Vote makes difference		Who is in power matters		Democratic satisfaction	
	(1)	(2)	(3)	(4)	(5)	(6)
Female	−0.033***	0.002	−0.045***	−0.017	−0.060***	−0.043***
	(0.009)	(0.012)	(0.009)	(0.012)	(0.009)	(0.012)
Low-skilled	−0.108***	−0.068***	−0.064***	−0.030**	−0.028***	−0.008
	(0.009)	(0.013)	(0.009)	(0.013)	(0.010)	(0.014)
Female X Low-skilled		−0.076***		−0.064***		−0.037**
		(0.018)		(0.017)		(0.018)
Education	0.137***	0.136***	0.092***	0.091***	0.078***	0.078***
	(0.004)	(0.004)	(0.004)	(0.004)	(0.004)	(0.004)
Household Income	0.072***	0.072***	0.079***	0.079***	0.114***	0.114***
	(0.004)	(0.004)	(0.004)	(0.004)	(0.004)	(0.004)
Political Ideology	0.029***	0.029***	0.025***	0.026***	0.056***	0.056***
	(0.002)	(0.002)	(0.002)	(0.002)	(0.002)	(0.002)
Age	0.031***	0.031***	0.013***	0.013***	0.017***	0.017***
	(0.003)	(0.003)	(0.003)	(0.003)	(0.003)	(0.003)
Unemployed	−0.141***	−0.142***	−0.112***	−0.113***	−0.225***	−0.225***
	(0.019)	(0.019)	(0.019)	(0.019)	(0.020)	(0.020)

Levels of Democracy	0.062***	0.063***	0.033***	0.034***	0.026***	0.027***
	(0.004)	(0.004)	(0.004)	(0.004)	(0.004)	(0.004)
GDP growth	−0.006***	−0.006***	0.004*	0.004*	0.031***	0.031***
	(0.002)	(0.002)	(0.002)	(0.002)	(0.002)	(0.002)
Intercept	−0.638***	−0.700***	−0.386***	−0.400***	−1.240***	−1.248***
	(0.080)	(0.080)	(0.094)	(0.094)	(0.167)	(0.168)
Random Effects						
Country-level Variance	0.236	0.236	0.377	0.376	1.396	1.398
	(0.486)	(0.486)	(0.614)	(0.613)	(1.182)	(1.182)
No. of Countries	52	52	52	52	52	52
No. of Individuals	250,553	250,553	250,553	250,553	250,553	250,553

Note: Multilevel logistic regression with random intercepts was used for all models. Standard errors are in parentheses. *** $p < 0.001$, ** $p < 0.01$, * $p < 0.5$.

matters, showing a higher level of skepticism toward politics. In addition, they are also less likely to be satisfied with the way democracy works in their countries. These findings confirm previous studies that precarious social and economic status negatively affects their political attitudes (Emmenegger et al., 2015; Kweon, 2018; Marx and Picot, 2013).

In this section, we argue that gender and class interact with one another in shaping voters' political attitudes. Specifically, our first two hypotheses predict that (1) the negative effect of working-class backgrounds on political efficacy will be bigger for women than men and that (2) the negative effect of working-class backgrounds on democratic satisfaction will be bigger for women than men. To test these hypotheses, we included an interaction term between respondents' gender and class. Columns (2), (4), and (6) present the coefficient results from the models with the interaction term. To help interpret these results, we visualized the marginal effect of low-skilled occupation by gender with 95% confidence intervals in Figures 15–17.

The figures show that while having a low-skilled occupation dampens political efficacy and democratic satisfaction, such a negative effect is stronger for women. Figure 15, for instance, shows that for male respondents, having a low-skilled occupation reduces the probability of believing that vote makes difference by about 7%. For female respondents, this figure is almost doubled to 14%.

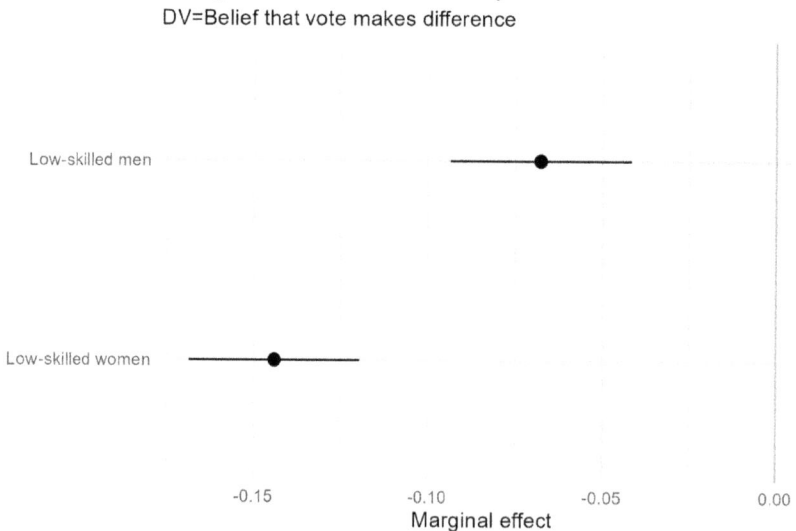

Figure 15 Marginal effect of low-skill on Pr (belief that vote makes difference)
Note: The figure is based on the model in column (2) in Table 9.

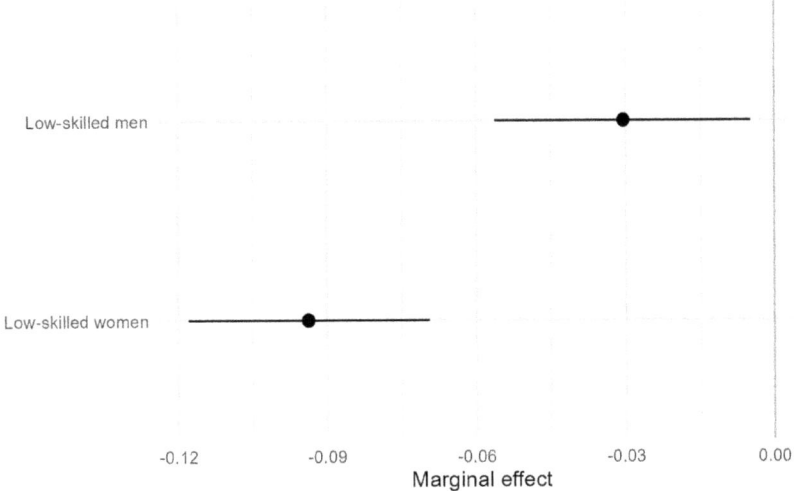

Figure 16 Marginal effect of low-skill on Pr (belief that who is in power matters)

Note: The figure is based on the model in column (4) in Table 9.

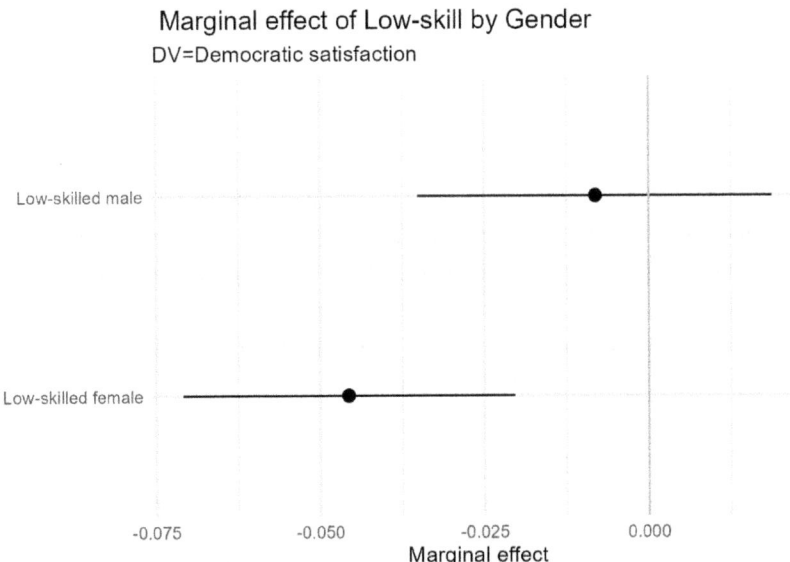

Figure 17 Marginal effect of low-skill on Pr (democratic satisfaction by gender)

Note: The figure is based on the model in column (6) in Table 9.

A similar effect is found for external efficacy as well. For male respondents, having a low-skilled occupation lowers the probability to belief that who is in power matters by about 3%, but for females, it reduces the probability by approximately 9%, showing the tripling effect. This indicates that low socioeconomic status has a more pronounced negative impact on women's internal efficacy compared to men's. A similar pattern is observed for external efficacy. Figure 15 illustrates that low-skilled occupational status negatively impacts both men's and women's external political efficacy, diminishing their belief that who is in power matters. However, this effect is significantly more pronounced for women than for men.

Beyond the effect on political efficacy, the economic marginalization of women has important implications for democracy. Figure 17 displays the marginal effect of low skill on the probability of being satisfied with the way democracy works in respondents' countries. The figure shows that for males, occupational status does not have much significant effect on their democratic satisfaction. In other words, the level of democratic satisfaction does not differ by occupation status for men. However, for females, having a low-skilled occupation has a negative impact on democratic satisfaction. Women with a low-skilled occupation, on average, have approximately a 4% lower probability to be satisfied with democracy than those with a high-skilled occupation. Given that women are overrepresented in low-skilled occupations in most countries, this finding raises a concern about the overall health of democracy.

4.5 Findings for Voting Behavior

We find that class has a gendered impact, with low-skilled occupational status exerting a more negative effect on women's political efficacy and satisfaction with democracy compared to men's. To further explore this dynamic, we examine whether these gendered effects extend to voting behavior. Specifically, we hypothesize that women from working-class backgrounds are more likely to abstain from voting than their male counterparts. Among those who do vote, we predict that a working-class background increases women's likelihood of supporting radical right-wing parties to a greater extent than it does for men.

Table 10 presents the results of our empirical analysis of voting behavior. Columns (1) and (2) report the effects on voting abstention, while columns (3) and (4) focus on support for radical right-wing parties. Columns (1) and (3) assess the independent effects of gender and economic class, without including an interaction term between the two variables. The findings indicate that gender alone does not have a significant direct effect on voting abstention – women are

Table 10 Effects on voting behavior

	Abstention		RRP Voting	
	(1)		(2)	
Female	0.018	0.009	−0.304***	−0.391***
	(0.012)	(0.016)	(0.023)	(0.032)
Low-skilled	0.183***	0.174***	0.139***	0.050
	(0.012)	(0.017)	(0.025)	(0.034)
Female X Low-skilled		0.018		0.186***
		(0.023)		(0.047)
Education	−0.228***	−0.228***	−0.027**	−0.025**
	(0.006)	(0.006)	(0.011)	(0.011)
Household Income	−0.135***	−0.135***	−0.113***	−0.113***
	(0.005)	(0.005)	(0.009)	(0.009)
Political Ideology	−0.025***	−0.025***	0.270***	0.270***
	(0.003)	(0.003)	(0.005)	(0.005)
Age	−0.242***	−0.242***	−0.033***	−0.033***
	(0.004)	(0.004)	(0.007)	(0.007)
Unemployed	0.242***	0.242***	0.224***	0.225***
	(0.023)	(0.023)	(0.056)	(0.056)
Levels of Democracy	0.259***	0.259***	0.069***	0.065***
	(0.007)	(0.007)	(0.015)	(0.015)
GDP Growth	−0.003	−0.003	−0.012**	−0.012**
	(0.003)	(0.003)	(0.006)	(0.006)
Intercept	−1.989***	−1.985***	−6.207***	−6.133***
	(0.175)	(0.176)	(0.598)	(0.622)
Random Effects				
Country-level Variance	1.414	1.414	11.360	11.360
	(1.189)	(1.189)	(3.370)	(3.370)
No. of Countries	54	54	35	35
No. of Individuals	249,995	249,995	137,478	137,478

Note: Multilevel logistic regression with random intercepts was used for all models. Standard errors are in parentheses. *** $p < 0.001$, ** $p < 0.01$, * $p < 0.5$.

no more likely than men to abstain from voting. However, occupational status plays a crucial role in shaping voting behavior. Individuals in low-skilled occupations are more likely to abstain from voting compared to those in high-skilled jobs. When it comes to supporting radical right-wing parties, both gender and class have significant effects. On average, women are less likely than men to vote for radical right-wing parties. In contrast, individuals in low-skilled occupations are more likely to support these parties compared to their high-skilled counterparts.

For our third and fourth hypotheses, we examine the interactive effects between gender and class, specifically focusing on whether the influence of class on voting behavior is greater for women than for men. To investigate this, we included an interaction term between gender and occupational class in our models. The results are reported in columns (2) and (4) of Table 10. To facilitate interpretation, we also visualized the findings in Figures 18 and 19 with 95% confidence intervals.

Figure 18 illustrates the marginal effects of having a low-skilled job on the probability of voting abstention. The figure demonstrates that for both men and women, having a low-skilled job significantly increases the likelihood of abstaining from voting. For men, a low-skilled job raises the probability of voting abstention by approximately 17%, while for women, the increase is slightly higher at nearly 19%. However, the impact of occupational status on men and women is not statistically distinguishable. In other words, the difference in the class effect on voting abstention between men and women is not statistically significant. This finding rejects our third hypothesis, which

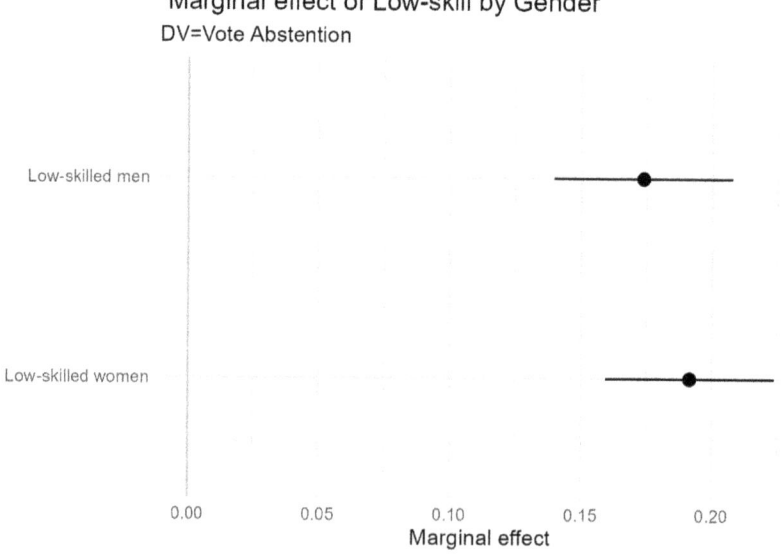

Figure 18 Marginal effects of low-skill on Pr (vote abstention)

Note: The figure is based on the model in column (2) in Table 10.

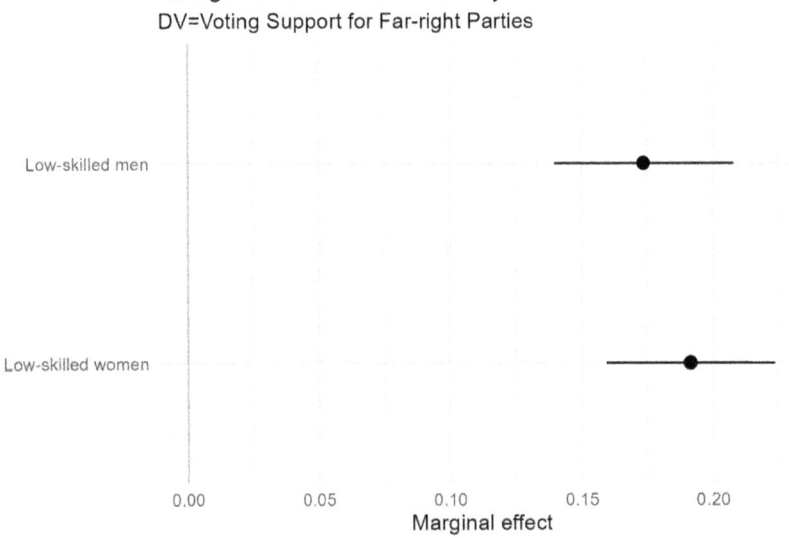

Figure 19 Marginal effects of low-skill on Pr (voting for far-right parties)
Note: The figure is based on the model in column (2) in Table 10.

predicted that the negative effect of working-class backgrounds on voting abstention would be greater for women than for men.

Figure 18 visualizes the marginal effects of having a low-skilled job on voting support for radical right-wing parties. Unlike the effects observed for voting abstention, the impact of class on support for radical right-wing parties shows significant gendered differences. The figure reveals that women with low-skilled occupations are significantly more likely to vote for radical right-wing parties compared to women in high-skilled occupations. Specifically, having a low-skilled job increases the likelihood of women voting for these parties by approximately 24%. For men, however, no such effect is observed; there is no statistically significant difference in their support for radical right-wing parties based on occupational status. This finding aligns with our fourth hypothesis, suggesting that class has a more pronounced effect on women's voting behavior than on men's. It highlights how disadvantaged economic status, represented by low-skilled occupations, influences women to engage in protest voting against the political establishment. These results underscore the gendered dynamics of class in shaping political behavior, particularly among those experiencing economic disadvantages.

In addition to the findings related to our key variables of interest, our analysis uncovers several interesting patterns in voting behavior. The results reveal that individuals with lower household incomes and lower levels of education are significantly more likely to abstain from voting and to support radical right-wing parties. These findings highlight the political disengagement and alignment with radical alternatives often observed among economically and socially disadvantaged groups. Moreover, ideological orientation plays a critical role. Ideologically conservative individuals are more likely to vote for radical right-wing parties. However, conservatives also exhibit higher voting turnout. Age is another important factor. Older individuals are more likely to participate in elections compared to younger voters, reflecting higher turnout rates. Interestingly, older voters are less likely to support radical right-wing parties, perhaps due to greater political stability or traditional partisan alignments among this demographic. Employment status also significantly influences voting behavior. The unemployed are more prone to abstain from voting and, when they do vote, are more likely to support radical right-wing parties. This suggests that economic precarity and disconnection from stable employment may drive both political disengagement and a turn toward radical political alternatives. Overall, these findings indicate that at the individual level, socially and economically marginalized groups are more inclined to withdraw from the electoral process and, when engaged, to express their dissatisfaction by supporting radical right-wing parties.

4.6 Summary and Implications

The analysis in this section highlights the interplay between socioeconomic class and gender in shaping political attitudes and behaviors. By integrating the two strands of literature on economic voting and gender representation, this section highlights how working-class backgrounds disproportionately disadvantage women compared to men, exerting a more significant influence on their political efficacy, democratic satisfaction, and voting behavior. We use post-election survey data from CSES to examine the interactive effects between class and gender on political behavior. The findings reveal that women in low-skilled occupations experience greater reductions in political efficacy and democratic satisfaction compared to their male counterparts. This suggests that the intersection of economic and gender-based disadvantages creates compounded barriers to political engagement for these women. For instance, while low-skilled occupations negatively affect the belief that one's vote matters and that political power is responsive, the impact is significantly greater for women. Similarly, low-skilled women report lower levels of satisfaction with democracy, reflecting broader disenfranchisement from the political system.

Class also exerts gendered impacts on voting patterns, extending beyond attitudes toward politics and the political system. In terms of voting behavior, the analysis uncovers significant gendered dynamics. While both men and women in low-skilled jobs are more likely to abstain from voting, the differences are not statistically significant. However, the findings show that women in low-skilled occupations are much more likely to support radical right-wing parties compared to their male counterparts. This aligns with the hypothesis that working-class women, facing systemic neglect and limited representation, may turn to anti-establishment parties as a form of protest voting. These results underscore the ways in which gender and class intersect to influence political participation, with marginalized women expressing their dissatisfaction through nontraditional political avenues.

The broader implications of these findings are significant, emphasizing the need for policies and interventions that address the intersection of socioeconomic and gender inequalities in politics. Efforts to enhance women's political representation should go beyond increasing their numerical presence and focus on addressing class inequalities, as these disparities have significant gendered impacts. The results further emphasize the importance of closing class-based gaps in representation among female politicians. Without addressing the priorities of working-class women, the disconnect between political institutions and marginalized groups is likely to persist, leaving working-class women increasingly disenfranchised with political systems.

The findings theoretically call for a re-evaluation of traditional approaches to understanding political behavior. By adopting an intersectional lens, this study highlights the complex ways in which multiple social identities interact to shape political attitudes. While prior research on gender and politics has primarily focused on the impact of gender on representation, intersectional analyses have often been limited to the interplay between gender and race. However, class emerges as another critical dimension with significant gendered implications for political behavior and attitudes. Unlike race, the effects of class transcend specific national contexts, making it a universal factor that warrants greater attention in studies of political behavior. Therefore, greater attention to the interaction between class and gender is essential for developing a more comprehensive understanding of gender inequalities in politics.

5 Conclusion

In this study, we have explored the complex interplay between class, gender, and political attitudes. Our analysis, spanning four sections, has delved into the nuanced ways in which socioeconomic status and gender intersect to shape individuals' perceptions of politics, efficacy, and democratic satisfaction. By examining the interaction between class and gender, we have uncovered significant theoretical and substantive implications that contribute to our understanding of political behavior and representation.

Specifically, Section 2 provides a comprehensive analysis of class and gender representation in contemporary democracies, focusing on the United States and the United Kingdom. By examining data from national legislatures, the section reveals pervasive patterns of underrepresentation, with white-collar backgrounds dominating over working-class backgrounds across both countries. Gendered disparities further compound these inequalities, with working-class women experiencing particularly low levels of descriptive representation. The analysis also highlights partisan differences in class representation, particularly among male legislators, suggesting a systemic marginalization of working-class women across political parties. These findings underscore the urgent need to address the representation gap, especially concerning working-class women, and emphasize the intersectional nature of political inequality. Moving forward, these insights inform broader discussions on democratic governance and policy outcomes, calling attention to the imperative of inclusive representation in shaping effective and equitable political systems. While Section 2 focuses on the descriptive and institutional dimensions of exclusion, Sections 3 and 4 turn to the subjective, attitudinal consequences of this exclusion – namely, how working-class women experience lower levels of trust, efficacy, and democratic satisfaction. Bridging these sections reveals an important area for future research: how underrepresentation itself may shape, reinforce, or exacerbate attitudinal alienation among multiply marginalized citizens. Studying this link more explicitly would deepen our understanding of the mechanisms through which institutional exclusion feeds political disaffection.

Section 3 delves into the theoretical framework, exploring how class and gender identities jointly shape policy preferences. It draws on previous research indicating that lower economic status and insecurity negatively impact political attitudes. Empirical findings corroborate these assertions, revealing that economic precarity diminishes political trust and efficacy, while insecure job conditions limit political participation. Moreover, the intersection of class and gender amplifies negative political attitudes among working-class women, who often face unique barriers due to their socioeconomic status and gender identity.

Section 4 further investigates the interaction of class and gender in shaping political attitudes and behaviors. The study hypothesizes that the negative impact of working-class backgrounds on political efficacy and democratic satisfaction is more pronounced for women than men. Empirical analyses confirm this hypothesis, demonstrating that women and working-class individuals exhibit lower political efficacy and democratic satisfaction compared to their counterparts. Moreover, the interaction of gender and class exacerbates these disparities, with low-skilled occupation having a stronger negative effect on political attitudes for women than men.

Our study makes several theoretical contributions to the existing literature on political attitudes and representation. First and foremost, we have utilized an intersectional approach to analyze how class and gender intersect to influence political attitudes. By adopting an intersectional lens, we move beyond simplistic analyses that treat class and gender as isolated factors and instead recognize their interconnectedness. This approach allows us to uncover the unique challenges faced by individuals occupying multiple marginalized identities, such as working-class women.

One theoretical contribution of this study is the recognition of the differential impact of socioeconomic status on political attitudes across gender lines. While previous research has often focused on either class or gender independently, our analysis demonstrates that the intersection of these identities produces distinct patterns of political behavior. Specifically, we find that working-class women experience compounded socioeconomic vulnerabilities, leading to heightened levels of political skepticism and dissatisfaction compared to their male counterparts. Differential lived experiences play a critical role in shaping individuals' policy preferences and political behavior. As shown in Figure 11, working-class women exhibit distinct policy preferences compared to their white-collar counterparts, whereas class appears to have a more limited effect on men's preferences. In terms of voting behavior, Figure 19 demonstrates that low-skilled women are more likely to support radical right-wing parties than white-collar women – a finding that both challenges and extends conventional class- or gender-based explanations in the literature. Together, these results underscore the importance of an intersectional approach in (re)interpreting long-standing empirical patterns in political behavior.

Furthermore, our study contributes to the literature on political representation by highlighting the differential effects of descriptive representation on diverse groups within society. We have demonstrated that while increased representation of certain social groups in politics may lead to greater political engagement and efficacy for those groups, it may simultaneously exacerbate feelings of exclusion and alienation among marginalized subgroups within those groups. This insight underscores the need for a more nuanced understanding of representation that takes into account intersecting identities and power dynamics.

Beyond its theoretical contributions, our study has substantive implications for both research and policy. One key implication is the importance of addressing the unique challenges faced by working-class women in political participation and representation. Our findings indicate that working-class women experience disproportionate economic challenges and gendered expectations that contribute to lower levels of political efficacy and democratic satisfaction. To address these disparities, targeted interventions are needed to enhance the political representation of working-class women and amplify their voices in the political arena.

The underrepresentation of working-class individuals, particularly women, in political office not only perpetuates inequalities but also undermines democratic legitimacy. To address this imbalance, efforts should be made to recruit and support candidates from diverse socioeconomic backgrounds, thereby ensuring that political institutions reflect the full spectrum of society. Increasing the diversity of political representatives to better reflect the socioeconomic and gender diversity of the population can, therefore, help bridge the representation gap and enhance political efficacy among marginalized groups.

There are several avenues for future research that warrant further exploration. One important direction for future research is to examine how other intersecting identities, such as race, ethnicity, and sexuality, interact with class and gender to shape political attitudes. Intersectionality is a multidimensional concept, and exploring the intersections of multiple identities can provide a more nuanced understanding of political behavior. Additionally, longitudinal studies are needed to examine how political attitudes and behavior evolve over time in response to changing socioeconomic and political contexts. Longitudinal data can help identify causal relationships between socioeconomic status, gender, and political attitudes, as well as track changes in political efficacy and satisfaction over time. Furthermore, comparative studies across different political contexts and cultural settings can help elucidate the ways in which class and gender intersect to shape political attitudes in diverse societies. By examining variation across countries and regions, researchers can identify common patterns as well as unique factors that influence political attitudes and representation.

References

Acker, Joan. 1990. "Hierarchies, jobs, bodies: A theory of gendered organizations." *Gender & society* 4(2): 139–158.

Andersen, Kristi. 1999. "The gender gap and experiences with the welfare state." *Political Science & Politics* 32(1): 17–19.

Andreoni, James, and Lise Vesterlund. 2001. "Which is the fair sex? Gender differences in altruism." *The Quarterly Journal of Economics* 116(1): 293–312.

Anzia, Sarah F., and Christopher R. Berry. 2011. "The Jackie (and Jill) Robinson effect: Why do congresswomen outperform congressmen?" *American Journal of Political Science* 55(3): 478–493.

Arulampalam, Wiji, Alison L. Booth, and Mark L. Bryan. 2007. "Is there a glass ceiling over Europe? Exploring the gender pay gap across the wage distribution." *ILR Review* 60(2): 163–186.

Atkeson, Lonna Rae. 2003. "Not all cues are created equal: The conditional impact of female candidates on political engagement." *Journal of Politics* 65(4): 1040–1061.

Atkeson, Lonna Rae, and Nancy Carrillo. 2007. "More is better: The influence of collective female descriptive representation on external efficacy." *Politics & Gender* 3: 79–101.

Atkinson, Mary Layton, and Jason Harold Windett. 2019. "Gender stereotypes and the policy priorities of women in Congress." *Political Behavior* 41(3): 769–789.

Barnes, Tiffany D., and Erin C. Cassese. 2017. "American party women: A look at the gender gap within parties." *Political Research Quarterly* 70(1): 127–141.

Barnes, Tiffany D., and Gregory W. Saxton. 2019. "Working-class legislators and perceptions of representation in Latin America." *Political Research Quarterly* 72(4): 910–928.

Barnes, Tiffany D., and Mirya R. Holman. 2020. "Essential worker is gender segregated: This shapes the gendered representation of essential workers in political office." *Social Science Quarterly* 101(5): 1827–1833.

Barnes, Tiffany D., and Stephanie M. Burchard. 2013. "Engendering politics: The impact of descriptive representation on women's political engagement in sub-Saharan Africa." *Comparative Political Studies* 46(7): 767–790.

Barnes, Tiffany D., Victoria D. Beall, and Mirya R. Holman. 2021. "Pink-collar representation and budgetary outcomes in US states." *Legislative Studies Quarterly* 46(1): 119–154.

Barnes, Tiffany D., Yann P. Kerevel, and Gregory W. Saxton. 2023. *Working Class Inclusion: Evaluations of Democratic Institutions in Latin America*. Cambridge: Cambridge University Press.

Barreto, Matt. 2010. *Ethnic Cues: The Role of Shared Ethnicity in Latino Political Participation*. Ann Arbor, MI: University of Michigan Press.

Bauer, Nichole M. 2020. *The Qualification Gap: Why Women Must Be Better Than Men to Win Political Office*. New York: Cambridge University Press.

Beauregard, Katrine. 2018. "Women's representation and gender gaps in political participation: Do time and success matter in a cross-national perspective?" *Politics, Groups, and Identities* 6(2): 237–263.

Bejarano, Christina, Nadia E. Brown, Sarah Allen Gershon, and Celeste Montoya. 2021. "Shared identities: Intersectionality, linked fate, and perceptions of political candidates." *Political Research Quarterly* 74(4): 970–985.

Bejarano, Christina E., Sylvia Manzano, and Celeste Montoya. 2011. "Tracking the Latino gender gap: Gender attitudes across sex, borders, and generations." *Politics & Gender* 7(4): 521–549.

Bernhard, Rachel, and Mirya R. Holman. 2025. *Gendered Jobs and Local Leaders: Women, Work, and the Pipeline to Local Political Office. Elements in Gender and Politics*. Cambridge: Cambridge University Press.

Betz, Timm, David Fortunato, and Diana Z. O'Brien. 2021. "Women's descriptive representation and gendered import tax discrimination." *American Political Science Review* 115(1): 307–315.

Betz, Timm, David Fortunato, and Diana Z. O'Brien. 2023. "Do women make more protectionist trade policy?" *American Political Science Review* 117(4): 1–9.

Blau, Francine D., and Lawrence M. Kahn. 1996. "Wage structure and gender earnings differentials: An international comparison." *Economica* 63(250): S29–S62.

Box-Steffensmeier, Janet M., Suzanna De Boef, and Tse-Min Lin. 2004. "The dynamics of the partisan gender gap." *American Political Science Review* 98(3): 515–528.

Brah, Avtar, and Ann Phoenix. 2004. "Ain't I a woman? Revisiting intersectionality." *Journal of International Women's Studies* 5(3): 75–86.

Campbell, David E., and Christina Wolbrecht. 2006. "See Jane run: Women politicians as role models for adolescents." *Journal of Politics* 68(2): 233–247.

Carnes, Nicholas. 2012. "Does the numerical underrepresentation of the working class in Congress matter?" *Legislative Studies Quarterly* 37(1): 5–34.

Carnes, Nicholas. 2013. *White-Collar Government: The Hidden Role of Class in Economic Policy Making*. Chicago: University of Chicago Press.

Carnes, Nicholas, and Noam Lupu. 2016. "Do voters dislike working-class candidates? Voter biases and the descriptive under-representation of the working class." *American Political Science Review* 110(4): 832–844.

Carnes, Nicholas, and Noam Lupu. 2015. "Rethinking the comparative perspective on class and representation: Evidence from Latin America." *American Journal of Political Science* 59(1): 1–18.

Cassese, Erin C., Heather L. Ondercin, and Jordan Randall. 2025. *Abortion Attitudes and Polarization in the American Electorate*. Cambridge: Cambridge University Press.

Celis, Karen, Sarah Childs, Johanna Kantola, and Mona Lena Krook. 2008. "Rethinking women's substantive representation." *Representation* 44(2): 99–110.

Chan, Tak Wing, and John H. Goldthorpe. 2007. "Class and status: The conceptual distinction and its empirical relevance." *American Sociological Review* 72(4): 512–532.

Charles, Maria, and David B. Grusky. 2005. *Occupational Ghettos: The Worldwide Segregation of Women and Men*. Vol. 200. Stanford: Stanford University Press.

Chi, Eunju, Yangho Rhee, and Hyeok Yong Kwon. 2013. "Inequality and political trust in Korea." *Korea Observer* 44(2): 199–222.

Clayton, Amanda, Diana Z. O'Brien, and Jennifer M. Piscopo. 2019. "All male panels? Representation and democratic legitimacy." *American Journal of Political Science* 63(1): 113–129.

Coffé, Hilde. 2019. "Gender, gendered personality traits and radical right populist voting." *Politics* 39(2): 170–185.

Cohen, Cathy. 2009. *The Boundaries of Blackness*. Chicago: University of Chicago Press.

Dahlerup, Drude, ed. 2005. *Women, Quotas and Politics*. New York: Routledge.

Dawson, Michael C. 1995. *Behind the Mule: Race and Class in African-American Politics*. Princeton: Princeton University Press.

Dietrich, Bryce J., Matthew Hayes, and Diana Z. O'Brien. 2019. "Pitch perfect: Vocal pitch and the emotional intensity of congressional speech." *American Political Science Review* 113(4): 941–962.

Dolan, Kathleen. 2003. *Voting for Women: How the Public Evaluates Women Candidates*. New York: Routledge.

Dolan, Kathleen. 2006. "Symbolic mobilization? The impact of candidate sex in American elections." *American Politics Research* 34(6): 687–704.

Durfee, Alesha, and Marcia K. Meyers. 2006. "Who gets what from government? Distributional consequences of child-care assistance policies." *Journal of Marriage and Family* 68(3): 733–748.

Eagly, Alice H., and Steven J. Karau. 2002. "Role congruity theory of prejudice toward female leaders." *Psychological Review* 109(3): 573–598.

Elsässer, Lea, and Armin Schäfer. 2022. "(N)one of us? The case for descriptive representation of the contemporary working class." *West European Politics* 45(6): 1361–1384.

Emmenegger, Patrick, Paul Marx, and Dominik Schraff. 2015. "Labour market disadvantage, political orientation and voting: How adverse labour market experiences translate into electoral behaviour." *Socio-Economic Review* 13(2): 189–213.

England, Paula. 2010. "The gender revolution: Uneven and stalled." *Gender & Society* 24(2): 149–166.

England, Paula. 2017. *Comparable Worth: Theories and Evidence*. New York: Routledge.

England, Paula, George Farkas, Barbara Stanek Kilbourne, and Thomas Dou. 1988. "Explaining occupational sex segregation and wages: Findings from a model with fixed effects." *American Sociological Review* 53(4): 544–558.

Evans, Geoffrey, and James Tilley. 2017. *The New Politics of Class: The Political Exclusion of the British Working Class*. Oxford: Oxford University Press.

Feldman, Stanley, and John Zaller. 1992. "The political culture of ambivalence: Ideological responses to the welfare state." *American Journal of Political Science* 36(1): 268–307.

Fernández, Juan J., and Antonio M. Jaime-Castillo. 2018. "The institutional foundation of social class differences in pro-redistribution attitudes: A cross-national analysis, 1985–2010." *Social Forces* 96(3): 1009–1038.

Funk, Patricia, and Christina Gathmann. 2015. "Gender gaps in policy making: Evidence from direct democracy in Switzerland." *Economic Policy* 30(81): 141–181.

Gay, Claudine. 2002. "Spiral of trust? The effect of descriptive representation on the relationship between citizens and their government." *American Journal of Political Science* 46(4): 717–732.

Gay, Claudine, and Katherine Tate. 1998. "Doubly bound: The impact of gender and race on the politics of Black women." *Political Psychology* 19(1): 169–184.

Gershon, Sarah Allen, Celeste Montoya, Christina Bejarano, and Nadia Brown. 2019. "Intersectional linked fate and political representation." *Politics, Groups, and Identities* 7(3): 642–653.

Gest, Justin, Tyler Reny, and Jeremy Mayer. 2018. "Roots of the radical right: Nostalgic deprivation in the United States and Britain." *Comparative Political Studies* 51(13): 1694–1719.

Gilens, Martin. 2009. *Why Americans Hate Welfare: Race, Media, and the Politics of Antipoverty Policy.* Chicago: University of Chicago Press.

Göbel, Sascha, and Simon Munzert. 2022. "The comparative legislators database." *British Journal of Political Science* 52(3): 1398–1408.

Goldin, Claudia. 1994. "Understanding the gender gap: An economic history of American women." In *Equal Employment Opportunity: Labor Market Discrimination and Public Policy*, 17–26.

Gray, Ron, and Elizabeth Francis. 2007. "The implications of US experiences with early childhood interventions for the UK Sure Start programme." *Child: Care, Health and Development* 33(6): 655–663.

Grumbach, Jacob M. 2015. "Does the American dream matter for members of Congress? Social-class backgrounds and roll-call votes." *Political Research Quarterly* 68(2): 306–323.

Gunderson, Morley. 1989. "Male-female wage differentials and policy responses." *Journal of Economic Literature* 27(1): 46–72.

Hancock, Ange-Marie. 2007. "When multiplication doesn't equal quick addition: Examining intersectionality as a research paradigm." *Perspectives on Politics* 5(1): 63–79.

Heath, Oliver. 2018. "Policy alienation, social alienation and working-class abstention in Britain, 1964–2010." *British Journal of Political Science* 48(4): 1053–1073.

Henry, P. J., Christine Reyna, and Bernard Weiner. 2004. "Hate welfare but help the poor: How the attributional content of stereotypes explains the paradox of reactions to the destitute in America." *Journal of Applied Social Psychology* 34(1): 34–58.

Herrera, Carlos, Geske Dijkstra, and Ruerd Ruben. 2019. "Gender segregation and income differences in Nicaragua." *Feminist Economics* 25(3): 144–170.

Herrnson, Paul S., J. Celeste Lay, and Atiya Kai Stokes. 2003. "Women running 'as women': Candidate gender, campaign issues, and voter-targeting strategies." *Journal of Politics* 65(1): 244–255.

Hoque, Kim, and Ian Kirkpatrick. 2003. "Non-standard employment in the management and professional workforce: Training, consultation and gender implications." *Work, Employment and Society* 17(4): 667–689.

Huddy, Leonie, Erin Cassese, and Mary-Kate Lizotte. 2008. "Gender, public opinion, and political reasoning." In Christina Wolbrecht, Karen Beckwith, and Lisa Baldez (Eds.) *Political Women and American Democracy* (pp. 31–49). Cambridge: Cambridge University Press.

Huffman, Matt L., and Steven C. Velasco. 1997. "When more is less: Sex composition, organizations, and earnings in US firms." *Work and Occupations* 24(2): 214–244.

Inglehart, Ronald, and Pippa Norris. 2003. *Rising Tide: Gender Equality and Cultural Change around the World*. Cambridge: Cambridge University Press.

Iversen, Torben, and Frances Rosenbluth. 2006. "The political economy of gender: Explaining cross-national variation in the gender division of labor and the gender voting gap." *American Journal of Political Science* 50(1): 1–19.

Iversen, Torben, and David Soskice. 2001. "An asset theory of social policy preferences." *American Political Science Review* 95(4): 875–893.

Javornik, Jana, and Anna Kurowska. 2017. "Work and care opportunities under different parental leave systems: Gender and class inequalities in Northern Europe." *Social Policy & Administration* 51(4): 617–637.

Jokela, Merita. 2019. "Patterns of precarious employment in a female-dominated sector in five welfare states – the case of paid domestic labor sector." *Social Politics: International Studies in Gender, State & Society* 26(1): 30–58.

Jones, Philip Edward. 2014. "Does the descriptive representation of gender influence accountability for substantive representation?" *Politics & Gender* 10(2): 175–199.

Jung, Jae-Hee, and Margit Tavits. 2024. *Counter-Stereotypes and Attitudes toward Gender and LGBTQ Equality*. Cambridge: Cambridge University Press.

Kalleberg, Arne L. 2012. "Job quality and precarious work: Clarifications, controversies, and challenges." *Work and Occupations* 39(4): 427–448.

Karp, Jeffrey A., and Susan A. Banducci. 2008. "Political efficacy and participation in twenty-seven democracies: How electoral systems shape political behaviour." *British Journal of Political Science* 38(2): 311–334.

Kerevel, Yann P., and Lonna Rae Atkeson. 2017. "Campaign, descriptive representation, quotas, and women's political engagement in Mexico." *Politics, Groups and Identities* 5(3): 454–477.

Kim, Jeong Hyun, and Yesola Kweon. 2024. "Double penalty? How candidate class and gender influence voter evaluations." *Research & Politics* 11(1): 1–9.

Kim, Young-Mi, and Sawako Shirahase. 2014. "Understanding intra-regional variation in gender inequality in East Asia: Decomposition of cross-national differences in the gender earnings gap." *International Sociology* 29(3): 229–248.

Kitschelt, Herbert, and Philipp Rehm. 2014. "Occupations as a site of political preference formation." *Comparative Political Studies* 47(12): 1670–1706.

Kittilson, Miki Caul. 2006. *Challenging Parties, Changing Parliaments: Women and Elected Office in Contemporary Western Europe*. Columbus: Ohio State University Press.

Kittilson, Miki Caul. 2016. "Gender and political behavior." In *Oxford Research Encyclopedia of Politics*. Oxford: Oxford University Press. Available at http://politics.oxfordre.com/view/10.1093/acrefore/9780190228637.001.0001/acrefore-9780190228637-e-71?print5pdf

Kittilson, Miki Caul, and Leslie A. Schwindt-Bayer. 2012. *The Gendered Effects of Electoral Institutions: Political Engagement and Participation.* New York: Oxford University Press.

Koenig, Anne M., Alice H. Eagly, Abigail A. Mitchell, and Tiina Ristikari. 2011. "Are leader stereotypes masculine? A meta-analysis of three research programs." *Psychological Bulletin* 137(4): 616–642.

Krook, Mona Lena. 2016. "Contesting gender quotas: Dynamics of resistance." *Politics, Groups, and Identities* 4(2): 268–283.

Kweon, Yesola. 2018. "Types of labor market policy and the electoral behavior of insecure workers." *Electoral Studies* 55: 1–10.

Kweon, Yesola. 2024. "We see symbols but not saviors: Women's representation and the political attitudes of working-class women." *Political Psychology* 45(2): 347–366.

Lawless, Jennifer L. 2015. "Female candidates and legislators." *Annual Review of Political Science* 18: 349–366.

Lazarus, Jeffrey, and Amy Steigerwalt. 2018. *Gendered Vulnerability: How Women Work Harder to Stay in Office.* Ann Arbor: University of Michigan Press.

Lee, Jiwon. 2023. "Consider your origins: Parental social class and preferences for redistribution in the United States from 1977 to 2018." *Social Science Research* 110: 102840.

Liu, Amy H., Roman Hlatky, Keith Padraic Chew, et al. 2025. *Gender, Ethnicity, and Intersectionality in Cabinets: Asia and Europe in Comparative Perspective.* Cambridge: Cambridge University Press.

Lizotte, Mary-Kate. 2022. "Public opinion and gender." In Thomas Rudolph (Ed.) *Handbook on Politics and Public Opinion* (pp. 193–207). Cheltenham: Edward Elgar Publishing.

Lizotte, Mary-Kate, and Tony E. Carey Jr. 2021. "Minding the Black gender gap: Gender differences in public opinion among Black Americans." *American Politics Research* 49(5): 490–503.

Lott, Bernice. 2002. "Cognitive and behavioral distancing from the poor." *American Psychologist* 57(2): 100–110.

Mandel, Hadas, and Michael Shalev. 2009. "Gender, class, and varieties of capitalism." *Social Politics* 16(2): 161–181.

Mansbridge, Jane. 1999. "Should blacks represent blacks and women represent women? A contingent 'yes'." *Journal of Politics* 61(3): 628–657.

Mansbridge, Jane, and Shauna L. Shames. 2008. "Toward a theory of backlash: Dynamic resistance and the central role of power." *Politics and Gender* 4(4): 623–634.

Manza, Jeff, and Clem Brooks. 2008. "Class and politics." In Annette Lareau, and Dalton Conley (Eds.) *Social Class: How Does It Work?* (pp. 201–231). New York: Russell Sage Foundation.

Marx, Paul. 2014. "Labour market risks and political preferences: The case of temporary employment." *European Journal of Political Research* 53(1): 136–159.

Marx, Paul, and Georg Picot. 2013. "The party preferences of atypical workers in Germany." *Journal of European Social Policy* 23(2): 164–178.

Matthews, Austin, S. and Yann Kerevel. 2022. "The nomination and electoral competitiveness of working class candidates in Germany." *German Politics* 31(3): 459–475.

McCall, Leslie. 2002. *Complex Inequality: Gender, Class and Race in the New Economy*. New York: Routledge.

McDermott, Monika L. 1998. "Race and gender cues in low-information elections." *Political Research Quarterly* 51(4): 895–918.

McLanahan, Sara, and Erin Kelly. 2006. "The feminization of poverty." In Janet Saltzman Chafetz *Handbook of the Sociology of Gender* (pp. 127–145). New York: Springer.

Mudde, Cas. 2007. *Populist Radical Right Parties in Europe*. New York: Cambridge University Press.

Mudde, Cas, and Cristóbal Rovira Kaltwasser. 2018. "Studying populism in comparative perspective: Reflections on the contemporary and future research agenda." *Comparative Political Studies* 51(13): 1667–1693.

Munger, Kevin. 2017. "Tweetment effects on the tweeted: Experimentally reducing racist harassment." *Political Behavior* 39(3): 629–649.

Murray, Rainbow. 2023. "It's a rich man's world: How class and glass ceilings intersect for UK parliamentary candidates." *International Political Science Review* 44(1): 13–26.

Niederle, Muriel, and Lise Vesterlund. 2007. "Do women shy away from competition? Do men compete too much?" *Quarterly Journal of Economics* 122(3): 1067–1101.

Norris, Mikel. 2015. "The economic roots of external efficacy: Assessing the relationship between external political efficacy and income inequality." *Canadian Journal of Political Science* 48(4): 791–813.

Norris, Pippa, and Joni Lovenduski. 1994. *Political Recruitment: Gender, Race and Class in the British Parliament*. Cambridge: Cambridge University Press.

O'Brien, Diana Z., and Jennifer Piscopo. 2018. "Electing women to national legislatures." In *Measuring Women's Political Representation across the Globe: Strategies, Challenges, and Future Research*, edited by Amy Alexander, Catherine Bolzendahl, and Farida Jalalzai, 139–164. Cham: Palgrave Macmillan.

O'Connor, Julia. 1993. "Gender, class, and citizenship in the comparative analysis of welfare state regimes: Theoretical and methodological issues." *British Journal of Sociology* 44(3): 501–518.

OECD. 2017. *The Pursuit of Gender Equality: An Uphill Battle*. Paris: OECD.

Oesch, Daniel. 2006. *Redrawing the Class Map: Stratification and Institutions in Britain, Germany, Sweden and Switzerland*. London: Palgrave Macmillan.

Oesch, Daniel. 2008. "The changing shape of class voting: An individual-level analysis of party support in Britain, Germany and Switzerland." *European Societies* 10(3): 329–355.

O'Grady, Tom. 2019. "Careerists versus coal-miners: Welfare reforms and the substantive representation of social groups in the British Labour Party." *Comparative Political Studies* 52(4): 544–578.

Oshri, Odelia, Liran Harsgor, Reut Itzkovitch-Malka, and Or Tuttnauer. 2022. "Risk aversion and the gender gap in the vote for populist radical right parties." *American Journal of Political Science* 66(4): 916–932.

Penn, Helen. 2007. "Childcare market management: How the United Kingdom government has reshaped its role in developing early childhood education and care." *Contemporary Issues in Early Childhood* 8(3): 192–207.

Phillips, Anne. 1995. *The Politics of Presence*. Oxford: Clarendon Press.

Phillips, Christian Dyogi 2021. *Nowhere to Run*. Oxford: Oxford University Press.

Philpot, Tasha S., and Hanes Walton Jr. 2007. "One of our own: Black female candidates and the voters who support them." *American Journal of Political Science* 51(1): 49–62.

Piketty, Thomas. 2014. *Capital in the Twenty-First Century*. Cambridge, MA: Harvard University Press.

Polachek, Solomon William. 1981. "Occupational self-selection: A human capital approach to sex differences in occupational structure." *Review of Economics and Statistics* 63(1): 60–69.

Rehm, Philipp. 2009. "Risks and redistribution: An individual-level analysis." *Comparative Political Studies* 42(7): 855–881.

Reingold, Beth, Kerry L. Haynie, and Kirsten Widner. 2020. *Race, Gender, and Political Representation*. Oxford: Oxford University Press.

Sandstrom, Heather, and Ajay Chaudry. 2012. "'You have to choose your childcare to fit your work': Childcare decision-making among low-income working families." *Journal of Children and Poverty* 18(2): 89–119.

Schraff, Dominik. 2017. "Labor market disadvantage and political alienation: A longitudinal perspective on the heterogeneous risk in temporary employment." *Acta Politica* 53(1): 48–67.

Schwindt-Bayer, Leslie A. 2010. *Political Power and Women's Representation in Latin America*. Oxford: Oxford University Press.

Schwindt-Bayer, Leslie A., and William Mishler. 2005. "An integrated model of women's representation." *Journal of Politics* 67(2): 407–428.

Simien, Evelyn M., and Rosalee A. Clawson. 2004. "The intersection of race and gender: An examination of Black feminist consciousness, race consciousness, and policy attitudes." *Social Science Quarterly* 85(3): 793–810.

Smooth, Wendy G. 2011. "Standing for women? which women? The substantive representation of women's interests and the research imperative of intersectionality." *Politics & Gender* 7(3): 436–441.

Spierings, Niels, and Andrej Zaslove. 2017. "Gender, populist attitudes, and voting: Explaining the gender gap in voting for populist radical right and populist radical left parties." *West European Politics* 40(4): 821–847.

Stauffer, Katelyn E. 2021. "Public perceptions of women's inclusion and feelings of political efficacy." *American Political Science Review* 115(4): 1226–1241.

Svallfors, Stefan. 2006. *The Moral Economy of Class: Class and Attitudes in Comparative Perspective*. Stanford: Stanford University Press.

Swers, Michele L. 2002. *The Difference Women Make: The Policy Impact of Women in Congress*. Chicago: University of Chicago Press.

Tate, Katherine. 1994. *From Protest to Politics: The New Black Voters in American Elections*. Cambridge, MA: Harvard University Press.

Taylor-Robinson, Michelle M., and Roseanna Michelle Heath. 2003. "Do women legislators have different policy priorities than their male colleagues? A critical case test." *Women & Politics* 24(4): 77–101.

Tomaskovic-Devey, Donald, Melvin Thomas, and Kecia Johnson. 2005. "Race and the accumulation of human capital across the career: A theoretical model and fixed-effects application." *American Journal of Sociology* 111(1): 58–89.

Verge, Tània, and María de la Fuente. 2014. "Playing with different cards: Party politics, gender quotas, and women's empowerment." *International Political Science Review* 35(1): 67–79.

Volden, Craig, Alan E. Wiseman, and Dana E. Wittmer. 2013. "When are women more effective lawmakers than men?" *American Journal of Political Science* 57(2): 326–341.

Weaver, R. Kent, Robert Y. Shapiro, and Lawrence R. Jacobs. 1995. "The polls – trends: Welfare." *Public Opinion Quarterly* 59(4): 606–627.

Wiener, Elizabeth. 2022. "Which women, exactly? Examining gender gaps in legislative responsiveness to women's issue advocacy through an intersectional lens." *Journal of Women, Politics & Policy* 43(1): 82–94.

Wolak, Jennifer. 2018. "Feelings of political efficacy in the fifty states." *Political Behavior* 40(3): 763–784.

Wolbrecht, Christina, and David E. Campbell. 2007. "Leading by example: Female members of parliament as political models." *American Journal of Political Science* 51(4): 921–939.

Wüest, Reto, and Jonas Pontusson. 2022. "Voter preferences as a source of descriptive (mis)representation by social class." *European Journal of Political Research* 61(2): 398–419.

Yildirim, Tevfik Murat. 2022. "Rethinking women's interests: An inductive and intersectional approach to defining women's policy priorities." *British Journal of Political Science* 52(3): 1240–1257.

Acknowledgement

This research was supported by the Yonsei University Research Grant of 2025.

Cambridge Elements

Gender and Politics

Tiffany D. Barnes
University of Texas at Austin

Tiffany D. Barnes is Professor of Political Science at the University of Texas at Austin. She is the author of *Women, Politics, and Power: A Global Perspective* (Rowman & Littlefield, 2007) and, award-winning, *Gendering Legislative Behavior* (Cambridge University Press, 2016). Her research has been funded by the National Science Foundation (NSF) and recognized with numerous awards. Barnes is the former president of the Midwest Women's Caucus and founder and director of the Empirical Study of Gender (EGEN) network.

Diana Z. O'Brien
Washington University in St. Louis

Diana Z. O'Brien is the Bela Kornitzer Distinguished Professor of Political Science at Washington University in St. Louis. She specializes in the causes and consequences of women's political representation. Her award-winning research has been supported by the NSF and published in leading political science journals. O'Brien has also served as a Fulbright Visiting Professor, an associate editor at *Politics & Gender*, the president of the Midwest Women's Caucus, and a founding member of the EGEN network.

About the Series

From campaigns and elections to policymaking and political conflict, gender pervades every facet of politics. Elements in Gender and Politics features carefully theorized, empirically rigorous scholarship on gender and politics. The Elements both offer new perspectives on foundational questions in the field and identify and address emerging research areas.

Cambridge Elements

Gender and Politics

Elements in the Series

In Love and at War: Marriage in Non-state Armed Groups
Hilary Matfess

Counter-Stereotypes and Attitudes Toward Gender and LGBTQ Equality
Jae-Hee Jung and Margit Tavits

The Politics of Bathroom Access and Exclusion in the United States
Sara Chatfield

Women, Gender, and Rebel Governance during Civil Wars
Meredith Maloof Loken

Abortion Attitudes and Polarization in the American Electorate
Erin C. Cassese, Heather L. Ondercin and Jordan Randall

Gender, Ethnicity, and Intersectionality in Cabinets: Asia and Europe in Comparative Perspective
Amy H. Liu, Roman Hlatky, Keith Padraic Chew, Eoin L. Power, Sam Selsky, Betty Compton and Meiying Xu

Gendered Jobs and Local Leaders: Women, Work, and the Pipeline to Local Political Office
Rachel Bernhard and Mirya R. Holman

What's Happened to the Gender Gap in Political Activity?: Social Structure, Politics, and Participation in the United States
Shauna L. Shames, Sara Morell, Ashley Jardina, Kay Lehman Schlozman and Nancy Burns

Family Matters: How Romantic Partners Shape Politicians' Careers
Olle Folke, Moa Frödin Gruneau and Johanna Rickne

Glass Ceilings, Glass Cliffs, and Quicksands: Gendered Party Leadership in Parliamentary Systems
Andrea S. Aldrich and Zeynep Somer-Topcu

Attitudes toward Political Authoritarianism in Economically Advanced Democracies: The Role of Gender Values and Norms
Amy C. Alexander and Gefjon Off

Double Glass Ceiling: The Class Effects of Gender Representation
Jeong Hyun Kim and Yesola Kweon

A full series listing is available at: www.cambridge.org/EGAP

For EU product safety concerns, contact us at Calle de José Abascal, 56–1°,
28003 Madrid, Spain or eugpsr@cambridge.org.

www.ingramcontent.com/pod-product-compliance
Ingram Content Group UK Ltd.
Pitfield, Milton Keynes, MK11 3LW, UK
UKHW020052230326
469195UK00017B/202